(C

Alleluia Verses and Tracts

For

Year C

Church Hymnal Series VI, Part III

Compiled By

Richard Crocker

For

The Standing Commission on Church Music

THE CHURCH HYMNAL CORPORATION
800 Second Avenue
New York, New York 10017

The Church Pension Fund
800 Second Avenue
New York, New York   10017

ISBN: 0-89869-064-1

GRADUAL PSALMS
ALLELUIA VERSES AND TRACTS

INTRODUCTION

An important aspect of liturgical renewal has been the increased use of psalmody in our worship. The three-year Eucharistic lectionary includes a wide selection of Psalms, providing possibilities for singing Psalms in various ways. This collection of Gradual Psalms, Alleluia Verses and Tracts consists of Psalm verses with Refrains, and provides an opportunity to participate in the ancient tradition of responsorial singing of the Psalms.

Psalmody at the gradual restores the tradition of having a cantor sing verses selected from a Psalm, while the congregation responds with a refrain; this tradition can be directly connected to Hebrew practice.

Proper Gregorian gradual melodies are usually extremely ornate, and unsuitable for typical modern parish use. In searching for a practical congregational psalmody, we turn to simpler, less elaborate Gregorian melodies. These have been preserved from ancient times, only in music for the offices (Matins, Lauds, Vespers, etc.) and not for the Holy Eucharist, and in the style of *antiphonal psalmody*, not *responsorial psalmody*. The solution to the problem of providing easily sung congregational gradual psalmody, as found in this collection, is to use the simpler forms and styles of office antiphonal psalmody, but having them sung by solo cantor and congregation in a responsorial style.

The compelling reason for doing this is the great value — practical, musical, and spiritual — of using these antiphon (refrain) melodies. They represent one of the most ancient traditions of Christian musical experience in a compact and accessible form. These priceless jewels of pure melody, many so short as to be sung in a single breath, seem to represent everything needed for our immediate purpose of congregational refrains for proper Psalms in the Eucharist.

The ancient repertory of Office antiphons (dating from the period circa A.D. 400-700), which is used as the source of the refrains in this collection, consists of melodies that are used again and again throughout

the Latin Office for many different texts. This fact
indicates that these antiphons are a broad, deep foun-
dation of Christian song. Because of this, it is rela-
tively easy to adapt these melodies for modern English
usage.

GUIDES FOR USE

A Psalm Tone has five parts, as shown in this
example:

TONE VI

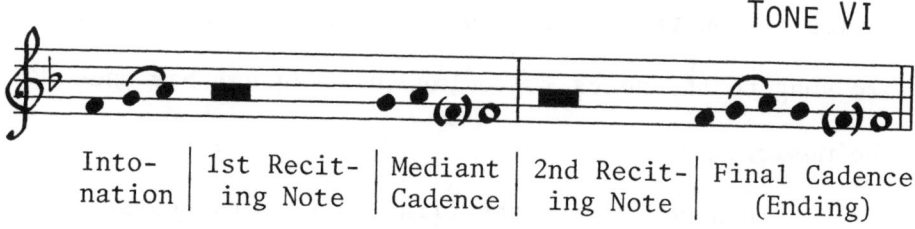

Into- nation	1st Recit- ing Note	Mediant Cadence	2nd Recit- ing Note	Final Cadence (Ending)

The *Intonation* is sung to the first two syllables
of each verse which follows the Refrain, and is indicated
in the text by italics. The Intonation is not sung at the
beginning of the second or third verse of a group of
verses.

The *1st Reciting Note* is used for all syllables
of the first half of the verse which are not sung to

the Intonation or to the Mediant Cadence, including
the initial syllables of the second or third verse of
a group of verses.

The *Mediant Cadence* comes before the asterisk
in the Psalm text, and consists of one or two accents,
and one, two, or three preparatory syllables. Accent
marks in the Psalm text (´) correspond to accent marks
under the notes in the Psalm Tone (♪). The notes in
parenthesis are used as needed between the syllables
with accent marks, or between the last accented syllable and the end of the half verse. Preparatory syllables follow the diagonal bar (/) in the text; they
are sung to the notes following the diagonal bar under
the music.

In a few cases, the first half of the verse
ends with an accented syllable. This should be sung to
the final accented note in the first half of the Psalm
Tone, omitting the note in parenthesis and the last
note of the Mediant Cadence. (When this happens, it is
considered an *abrupt mediation.*)

In some Psalm Tones, two (and in some cases,
three or four) notes are slurred together. These should

never be divided between two syllables. Words or syllables requiring two or more notes are indicated by dots over the syllables in the pointed text (e.g., set up-ȯn your thröne [for Psalm Tone I *d*]).

The *2nd Reciting Note* is used like the first, and the *Final Cadence* is used like the *Mediant Cadence*.

In a few cases, due to the shortness of the half verse, the Intonation or the Reciting Note is omitted. This is indicated in the pointed text by the use of a dash (——) (e.g., O LȮRD —— God óf hosts).

In some cases, it has not been possible to align the real accents of the English text with the accented notes of the Psalm Tone. In such cases, the accent marks over the syllables in the pointed text indicate how the syllable goes with the notes.

+ + + +

The Refrain and Psalm Tone are sung in the following manner:

1. The Refrain is sung first by a cantor.
2. The Refrain is then immediately repeated by the congregation and choir.
3. Each Psalm verse, or group of verses, is sung by the cantor.
4. The Refrain is repeated by the congregation and choir after each verse or group of verses, as indicated in the pointed text.

The Alleluia with its Verses is sung in a similar
manner:

1. The Alleluia is sung first by a cantor.
2. The Alleluia is then repeated by the congregation and choir.
3. The Verse is sung by the cantor.
4. The Alleluia is repeated by the congregation
   and choir.

The Tract may be sung by the cantor throughout; or

begun by the cantor and continued by the congregation

and choir.

The Refrains should be sung in a natural,

flowing manner, without undue accents or change of pace.

They can be faster or slower, or otherwise varying in

character according to the text, the season, or the oc-

casion. Many Refrains can be sung as one phrase without

stopping for breath. Others have a natural division of

sense, marked in the music by a half bar, where a breath

may be taken. Refrains should follow the Psalm verses

without hesitation.

Choosing a comfortable pitch for both cantor

and the people is very important. In this collection,

Refrains and Psalm Tones often have been transposed into

a comfortable range, but additional transpositions might

be necessary.

The Gradual Psalm could be thought of as a second Old Testament reading, which is normally sung rather than read, and the people's response to this reading is the Refrain. The cantor should sing the Psalm verses in full view of the congregation, from the lectern or pulpit, or from some other visible location where the other lessons are read. The congregation should remain seated for the Gradual Psalm, as they do for other readings. The Gloria Patri is not added to the Gradual Psalm verses, since this is a continuation of the reading from the Old Testament.

The Alleluia Verse (or Tract) may be sung by the cantor from the choir, and may follow or be followed by a hymn. The congregation stands for the singing of the Alleluia (and hymn) and remains standing for the Gospel.

The Refrains, Verses, Alleluias and Tracts are normally sung without accompaniment, but a convenient manner of performance in many parishes and missions would be to have the organ (or other instrument) play the complete Refrain or Alleluia melody before it is sung by the cantor. It is then sung by the cantor alone, then repeated by congregation and choir, and continued according to the directions above. It might be helpful for the organ (or other instrument) to play the Refrain in unison octaves while the congregation sings, until the melody is known well enough to be sung without instrumental assistance. In some situations, it might be possible to ring bells during Refrains and Alleluias, either in a set pattern, or at random. The verses should be sung without any accompaniment.

In some places, and during certain times of the year, it may be preferable to have the verses sung by two or three cantors, or even by the entire choir. When the people have become familiar with this style of singing the Psalm verses, it might be desirable to urge the entire congregation to join in singing the verses as well as the Refrains and Alleluias.

As in other parts of the Eucharist, the use of psalmody in the Service of the Word allows flexibility and a freedom of choice: the text for the Refrains is not a part of the Lectionary, and other Refrains and Psalm verses may be used in place of the ones used in this collection. While the shorter selection of verses, as found in the Lectionary, is usually sung at the Gradual in the Eucharist, in some situations a larger part of the Psalm, or the entire Psalm, may be sung. Some congregations may wish to sing a seasonal Refrain, using the same Refrain — words and music — throughout a season of the Church Year. In other places, it might be preferable to repeat the same Gradual Psalm through-out a particular season. Other musical forms and styles, or course, may be used in the singing of both Refrains and Verses. Some congregations may wish to use harmo-nized chant (Anglican Chant) for the Verses with the Refrains in unison; in other places, forms of modern chant may be used; in still other congregations, the Psalms may be sung in metrical versions.

This collection provides music which has been sung by the Church for many centuries, and it is hoped that this music will continue to be sung for years to come. Through the use of these ancient Refrains and Psalm Tones, it is hoped that the contemporary and future Church will look upon this traditional song of the Church not only as a fitting way to sing the Psalms,

but also as a model and inspiration for the creation of
new liturgical psalmody.

The complete Gradual Psalms will appear as
Church Hymnal Series VI in the following parts:

Part I   - Year A
Part II   - Year B
Part III - Year C
Part IV   - Holy Days, The Common of Saints
             and for Various Occasions
Part V   - *Lesser Feasts and Fasts* and
             selected Psalms from *The Book
             of Occasional Services*

These Psalms will be issued in the following order:

Part I
Part IV
Part II
Part III
Part V

The Standing Commission on Church Music expresses
deepest appreciation to the many congregations, clergy
and musicians who have included representative items
from this collection in their services, and have offered
many helpful suggestions, many of which have been incor-
porated in this publication. We are especially grateful
to Dr. Richard Crocker for his research and preparation
of the psalmody and for his assistance in the preparation

of the introduction to the collection. The Refrain texts represent the research and work of Captain Howard Galley, C.A.. The Commission is most grateful to him, to members of the Standing Commission on Church Music Service Music Committee, and to the Reverend Ronald V. Haizlip who prepared the manuscript which has been used for this publication of the psalmody.

1 ADVENT C

REFRAIN

Out of Zi-on, per-fect in its beau-ty,

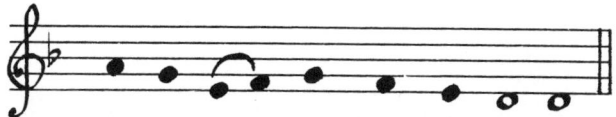

God re-veals him-self in glo-ry.

PSALM 50

TONE I*f*

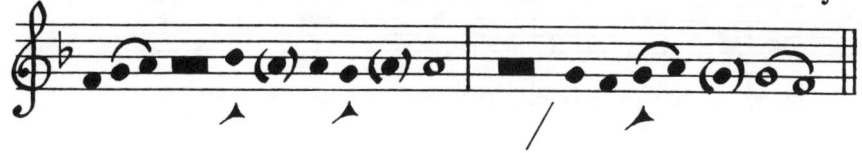

1 *The LÖRD*, the God of góds, has spó-ken;*
      he has called the earth from the rising of
                              the sun / to its sët-tiṅg.
2 Out of Zion, perfect íń its béau-ty,*
      God reveals him - / self in gĺo-rÿ.

REFRAIN

3 *Our Göd* will come and will nót keep sí-lence;*
      before him there is a consuming flame,
      and round about / him a räg-ing störm.
4 He calls the heavens and the eárth from á-bove*
      to witness the judgment / of his péö-ṗle.

REFRAIN

5 "*Ga-thёr* before me my lóy-al fól-low-ers,*
      those who have made a covenant with me
      and sealed / it with säc-ri-fiče."
6 Let the heavens declare the ríght-ness óf his cause;*
      for / God him-šëlf is jüdge.

REFRAIN

1 Advent C

Alleluia VIII

Al-le - lu - ia, al-le-lu - ia, al - le-lu-ia.

Verse (Psalm 85:7)   Tone VIII*g*

Show us your mercy, O Lord,*   and grant us

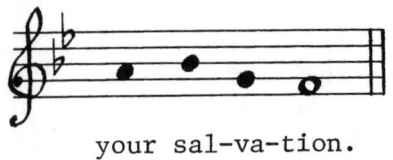

your sal-va-tion.

REFRAIN

The Lord has done great things for us,

and we are glad in - deed.

PSALM 126   TONE I$_g$

1 *When the* LORD restored the fór-tunes of Zí-on,*
   then were / we like thóse who dream.
2 Then was our mouth fílled with laúgh-ter,*
   and our / tongue with shóuts of joy.

                                        REFRAIN

3 *Then they* said a-móng the ná-tions,*
   "The LORD has / done great thíngs for them."
4 The LORD has dóne great thíngs for us,*
   and / we are glád in-deed.

                                        REFRAIN

5 *Re - store* our fór-tunes, Ó LORD,*
   like the watercourses / of the Ñe-gev.
6 —— Thóse who sowed with tears*
   will / reap with sóngs of joy.

                                        REFRAIN

7 *Those who* go out weeping, cár-ry-íng the seed,*
   will come again with joy, / shoul-der-íng
                          their sheaves.

                                        REFRAIN

BCP, p. 782

2 ADVENT C

ALLELUIA I

Al-le-lu - ia, al-le-lu - ia,   al-le - lu-ia.

VERSE   (Luke 3:4,6)   TONE I*f*

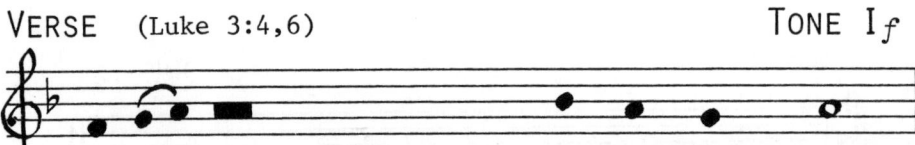

Pre-pare the way of the Lord, make his paths straight;*

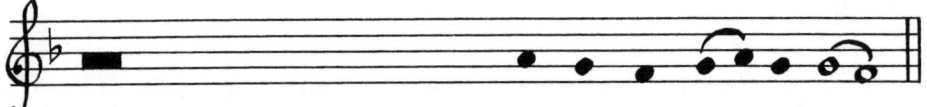

and all flesh shall see the sal-va-tion of   our God.

3 ADVENT C

REFRAIN

Ring out your joy, in-hab-i-tants of Zi-on;

the Ho-ly One of Is-ra-el is in the midst of you.

CANTICLE 9 (Isaiah 12:2-6)   TONE IV*a*

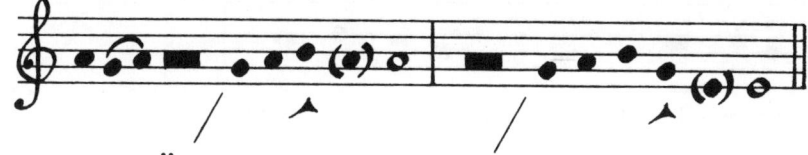

1 *Sure-ly*, it is / God who sáves me;*
  I will trust in / him and not bé a-fraid.
2 For the Lord is my stronghold / and my súre de-fense,*
  and he / will be my Sáv-ior.

                                    REFRAIN

3 *There-fore* you shall draw water / with re-jóic-ing*
  from the / springs of sal-vá-tion.
4 And on that day / you shall sáy,*
  Give thanks to the Lord and / call up-on hís Name;

                                    REFRAIN

5 *Make his* deeds known a - / mong the péo-ples;*
  see that they remember that his / Name is ex-ált-ed.
6 Sing the praises of the Lord, for / he has dóne
                            great things,*
  and this is / known in all thé world.

                                    REFRAIN

7 *Cry a* - loud, inhabitants of Zion, ring / out your jóy,*
  for the great one in the midst of you is
                        the Holy / One of Is-rá-el.

                                    REFRAIN

BCP, p. 86

3 ADVENT C

ALLELUIA IV

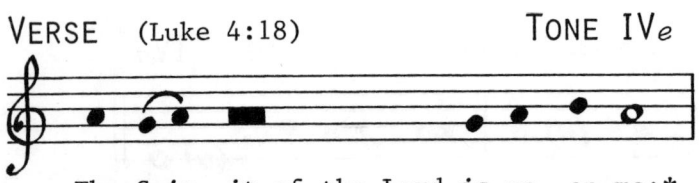

Al-le-lu-ia, al-le - lu - ia, al-le - lu-ia.

VERSE   (Luke 4:18)   TONE IVe

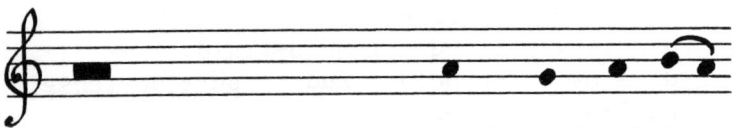

The Spir - it of the Lord is up - on me;*

he has anointed me to preach good tid-ings

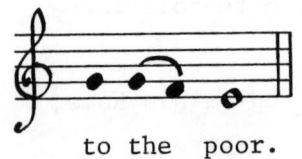

to the   poor.

3 ADVENT C

REFRAIN

Show us your mer - cy, O Lord,

and grant us your sal-va - tion.

PSALM 85   TONE I*f*

8 *I will* listen to what the LORD Gód is sáy-ing,*
    for he is speaking peace to his faithful people
    and to those who / turn their héarts to him.
9 Truly, his salvation is very near to thóse who féar him,
    that his glory may / dwell in óur land.

                            REFRAIN

10 *Mer - cy* and truth have mét to-géth-er;*
     righteousness and peace have / kissed each óth-ér.
11 Truth shall spring úp from thé earth,*
     and righteousness shall look / down from héav-én.

                            REFRAIN

12 *The LORD* will indeed gránt pros-pér-i-ty,*
     and our land will / yield its ín-creáse.
13 Righteousness shall gó be-fóre him,*
     and peace shall be a / path-way fór his feét.

                            REFRAIN

3 ADVENT C

ALLELUIA IV

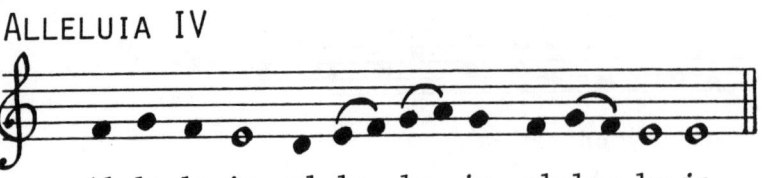

Al-le-lu-ia, al-le - lu - ia, al-le - lu-ia.

VERSE (Luke 4:18)   TONE IV*e*

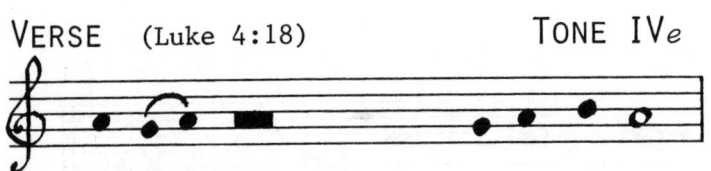

The Spir - it of the Lord is up - on me;*

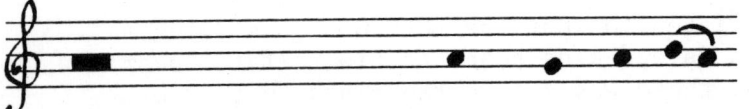

he has anointed me to preach good tid-ings

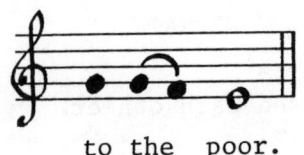

to the poor.

REFRAIN

Re-store us, O God of hosts; show the light

of your coun-te-nance and we shall be saved.

PSALM 80   TONE I*g*

1 *Hear, Ȯ̇* Shepherd of Israel, leading Jó-seph líke
                              a flock;*
    shine forth, you that are enthroned up - / on the
                          chér̈-u-bim.
2 In the presence of Ephraim, Benjamin, añd Ma-nás-seh,*
    stir up your strength, and / come to hélp us.

                                              REFRAIN

4 *O LȮ̇RD* —— Gód óf hosts,*
    how long will you be angered
    despite the prayers / of your péö-ple?
14 Turn now, O God of hosts, look down from heaven;
    be-hóld and ténd this vine;*
    preserve what your right / hand has pláñt-ed.

                                              REFRAIN

16 *Let yöur* hand be upon the mán of your ríght hand,*
    the son of man you have made so / strong for
                          yóür-self.
17 And so we will never túrn a-wáy from you;*
    give us life, that we may / call up-óñ your Name.

                                              REFRAIN

                                        BCP, p. 702

4 ADVENT C

ALLELUIA III

Al-le - lu - ia, al-le - lu-ia, al-le - lu-ia.

VERSE (Luke 1:38)   TONE IIIa

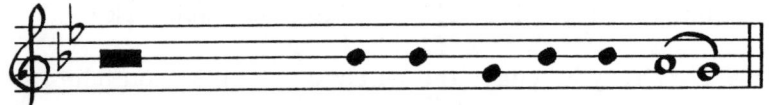

Be - hold, I am the hand-maid of the Lord;*

let it be to me ac-cord-ing to your word.

CHRISTMAS DAY ABC I   *(at midnight)*

REFRAIN

To-day is born our Sav-ior, Christ the Lord.

PSALM 96   TONE V*a*

1   *Sing to* the LORD a néw song;*
      sing to the LORD, áll the whóle earth.
2   Sing to the LORD and bléss his Name;*
      proclaim the good news of his sal-vá-tion
                              from dáy to day.
                                              REFRAIN

3   *De - clare* his glory among the ná-tions*
      and his wonders a-móng all péo-ples.
4   For great is the LORD and greatly to be praísed;*
      he is more to be feáred than áll gods.

                                              REFRAIN

11 *Let the* heavens rejoice, and let the earth be glad;
      let the sea thunder and all that is ín it;*
      let the field be joyful and áll that ís there-in.

                                              REFRAIN

12 *Then shall* all the trees of the wood shout for joy
      before the LORD when he cómes,*
      when he cómes to júdge the earth.

                                              REFRAIN

CHRISTMAS DAY ABC I   *(at midnight)*

ALLELUIA VIII

Al-le - lu - ia, al-le-lu - ia, al - le-lu-ia.

VERSE   (Luke 2:10-11)   TONE VIIIg

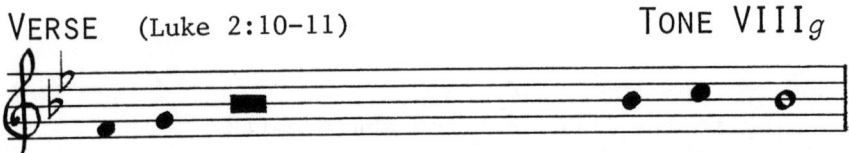

Be-hold, I bring you good tidings of great joy;*

to you is born a Sav-ior, Christ the Lord.

CHRISTMAS DAY ABC II   *(at dawn)*

REFRAIN

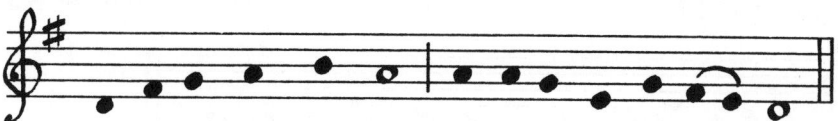

To us a child is born; to us a Son is giv-en.

PSALM 97   TONE VIIb

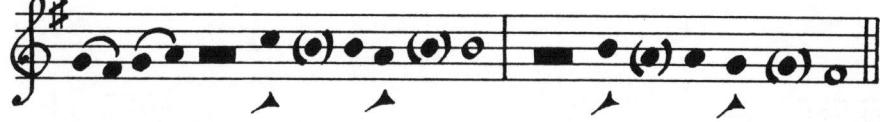

1 *The LORD* is King;
     lét the eárth re-joice;*
        let the multitude óf the ísles be glad.
2 Clouds and darkness are roúnd a-bóut him,*
        righteousness and justice are the foun-dá-tions
                        óf his throne.
                                            REFRAIN

3 *A fire* —— góes be-fóre him*
        and burns up his ene-míes on év-ery side.
4 His líght-nings light úp the world;*
        the earth seés it and ís a-fraid.
                                            REFRAIN

11 *Light has* sprung úp for the ríght-eous,*
        and joyful gladness for those who afe true-heárt-ed.
12 Rejoice in the LÓRD, you ríght-eous,*
        and give thánks to his hó-ly Name.
                                            REFRAIN

ALLELUIA II

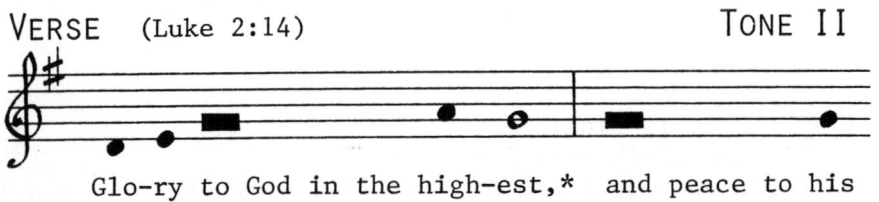

Al – le-lu-ia, al-le-lu-ia, al-le-lu-ia.

VERSE   (Luke 2:14)   TONE II

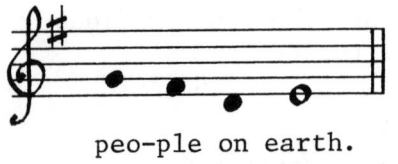

Glo-ry to God in the high-est,*   and peace to his

peo-ple on earth.

CHRISTMAS DAY ABC III (during the day)

REFRAIN

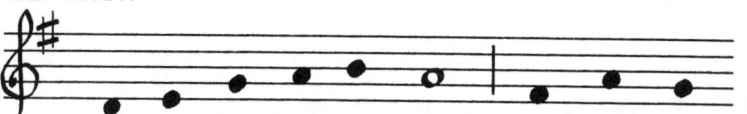

All the ends of the earth have seen the

sal-va-tion of our God.

PSALM 98   TONE VIIa

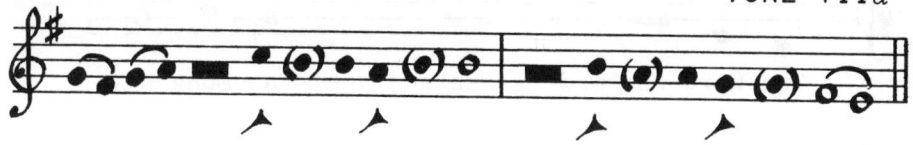

1 Sing to the LORD a new song,*
   for he has done mar-ve-lous things.
2 With his right hand and his ho-ly arm*
   has he won for him-self the vic-to-ry.

                                          REFRAIN

3 The LORD has made known his vic-to-ry;*
   his righteousness has he openly shown in
                 the sight of the na-tions.
4 He remembers his mercy and faithfulness to
                 the house of Is-ra-el,*
   and all the ends of the earth have seen the
                 vic-to-ry of our God.

                                          REFRAIN

5 Shout with joy to the LORD, all you lands;*
   lift up your voice, re-joice, and sing.
6 Sing to the LORD with the harp,*
   with the harp and the voice of song.

                                          REFRAIN

CHRISTMAS DAY ABC III   *(during the day)*

ALLELUIA II

Al - le-lu-ia, al-le-lu-ia, al-le-lu-ia.

VERSE   (John 1:14)   TONE II

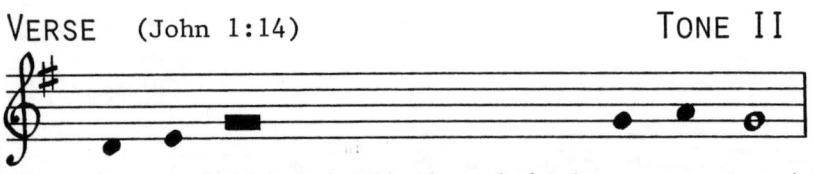

The Word was made flesh and dwelt a - mong us,*

full of grace and truth.

1 CHRISTMAS ABC

REFRAIN

The Word was made flesh and dwelt a - mong us.

PSALM 147   TONE VIIb

13 *Wör - ship* the LORD, O Je-rú-sa-lem;*
     praise your Gód, O Zí-on;
14 For he has strengthened the bárs of yoúr gates;*
     he has blessed your chíl-dren with-iń you.

                                                           REFRAIN

15 *He has* established peáce on your bór-ders;*
     he satisfies you with the fín-est wheat.
16 He sends out his com-mánd to thé earth,*
     and his word runs vé-ry swíft-ly.

                                                           REFRAIN

20 *He de* - clares his wórd to Já-cob,*
     his statutes and his júdg-ments to Iś-ra-el.
21 He has not done so to any óth-er ná-tion;*
     to them he has not revealed his judgments.
     Hál-le-lú-jah!

                                                           REFRAIN

ALLELUIA II

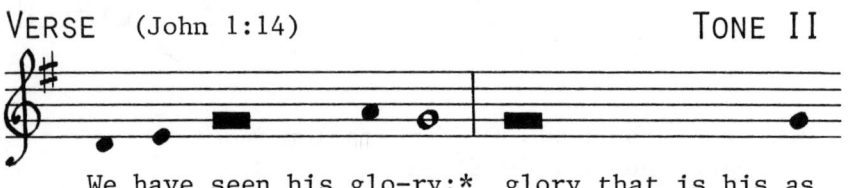

Al - le-lu-ia, al-le-lu-ia, al-le-lu-ia.

VERSE (John 1:14)   TONE II

We have seen his glo-ry;* glory that is his as

the Fa-ther's on-ly Son.

HOLY NAME ABC

REFRAIN

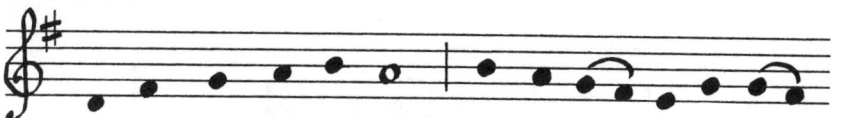

O Lord our Gov-er-nor, how ex-alt-ed is your

Name in all the world!

PSALM 8

TONE VIIb

4 *When I* consider your heavens, the wórk of your fín-gers,*
   the moon and the stars you have sét in their cóur-ses,
5 What is man that you should be mínd-ful óf him?*
   the son of man that yóu should seék him out?

REFRAIN

6 *You have* made him but little lower thán the án-gels;*
   you adorn him with gló-ry and hón-or;
7 You give him mastery over the wórks of yóur hands;*
   you put all things ún-der hís feet:

REFRAIN

8 —— All sheép and óx-en,*
   even the wild beásts of thé field,
9 The birds of the air, the fiśh of thé sea,*
   and whatsoever walks in the páths of thé sea.

REFRAIN

BCP, p. 592

HOLY NAME ABC

ALLELUIA I

Al-le-lu - ia, al-le-lu - ia,   al-le - lu-ia.

VERSE   (Hebrews 1:1-2)   TONE I*f*

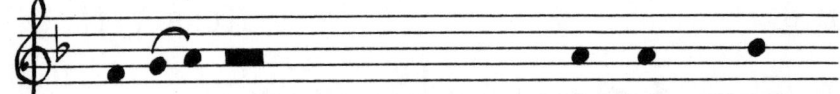

In the   past God spoke to our fa-thers through

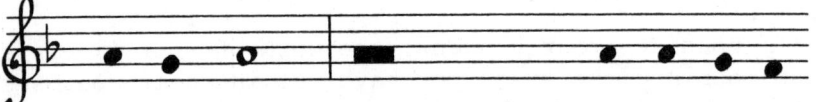

the pro-phets,*   but now he has spo-ken to us

through his Son.

REFRAIN

How dear to me is your dwell-ing, O Lord of hosts!

PSALM 84   TONE VIIb

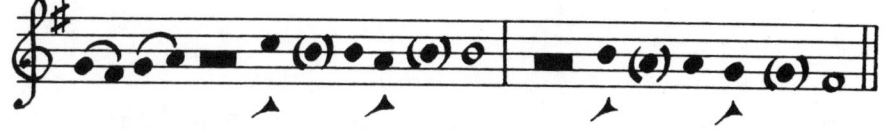

1 *My soul* has a desire and longing for the coúrts of
                    thé LORD;*
   my heart and my flesh re-jóice in the lív-ing God.
2 The sparrow has found her a house
   and the swallow a nest where shé may láy her young;*
      by the side of your altars, O LORD of hosts,
      my Kíng and mý God.

                                              REFRAIN

3 *Hap-py* are they who dwéll in yóur house!*
   they will ál-ways be práis-ing you.
4 Happy are the people whose stréngth is iń you!*
   whose hearts are sét on the píl-grims' way.

                                              REFRAIN

5 *Those who* go through the desolate valley will fińd
                    it a pláce of springs,*
   for the early rains have covered it with
                    poóls of wá-ter.
6 They will climb from héight to height,*
   and the God of gods will reveal him-sélf in Zí-on.

                                              REFRAIN

7 *LORD God* of hósts, hear mý prayer;*
   hearken, O Gód of Já-cob.
8 Behold our de-fénd-er, Ó God;*
   and look upon the face of yóur A-nóint-ed.

                                              REFRAIN

BCP, p. 707

ALLELUIA II

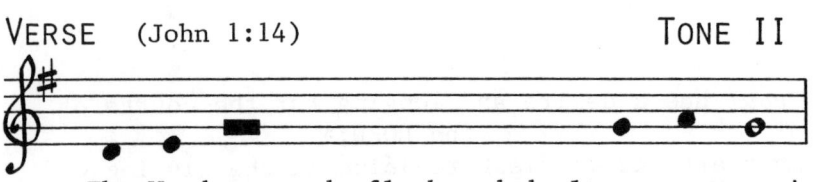

Al - le-lu-ia, al-le-lu-ia, al-le-lu-ia.

VERSE   (John 1:14)   TONE II

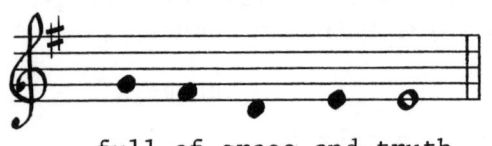

The Word was made flesh and dwelt a - mong us,*

full of grace and truth.

EPIPHANY ABC

REFRAIN

All kings shall bow down be-fore him;

all the na-tions shall do him ser-vice.

PSALM 72   TONE VII♭

1 *Gíve thè* King your jús-tice, Ó God,
   and your righteousness tó the Kíng's Son;
2 That he may rule your péo-ple ríght-eous-ly*
   and the poór with jús-tice;

                                    REFRAIN

8 *Hè shäll* —— rúle from séa to sea,*
   and from the River to the eńds of thé earth.
10 The kings of Tarshish and of the ísles shall
                    pay tríb-ute,*
   and the kings of Arabia and Sá-ba óf-fer gifts.

                                    REFRAIN

12 *För hè* shall deliver the poor who crîes out iń dis-tress,*
   and the oppressed who hás no hélp-er.
13 He shall have pity on the lów-ly ańd poor;*
   he shall preserve the líves of the néed-y.

                                    REFRAIN

17 *Mäy hìs* Name remain for ever
   and be established as lóng as the sún en-dures;*
   may all the nations bless themselves in him and
                    cáll him bléss-ed.

                                    REFRAIN

                                    BCP, p. 685

EPIPHANY ABC

ALLELUIA II

Al - le-lu-ia, al-le-lu-ia, al-le-lu-ia.

VERSE (Matt. 2:2)   TONE II

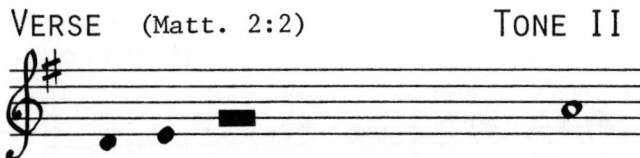

We have seen his star in the East,*

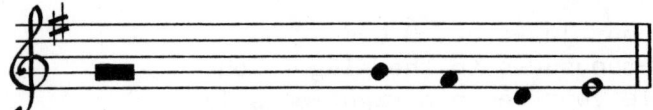

and have come to wor-ship the Lord.

1 Epiphany ABC

Refrain

I have found Da-vid my ser-vant; with my

ho-ly oil have I   a-noint-ed him.

Psalm 89   Tone I*f*

21 *My hand* will hóld hím fast*
      and my / arm will máke him stróng.
22 No enemy sháll de-céive him*
      nor any wicked / man bring hím dówn.

                                          REFRAIN

24 *My faith* - fulness and lóve shall bé with him,*
      and he shall be victori - / ous through my̎ Name.
25 I shall make his do-mín-ion éx-tend*
      from the Great Sea / to the Rív-er̈.

                                          REFRAIN

26 *He will* say to me, 'Yóu are my Fá-ther,*
      my God, and the rock of / my sal-v̎ä-tiön.'
27 I will make him my fíŕst-born*
      and higher than the / kings of the earth.

                                          REFRAIN

28 *I will* keep my love for hím for év-er,*
      and my covenant / will stand fir̎m for him.
29 I will establish his líne for év-er*
      and his throne as the / days of héäv-en̈.

                                          REFRAIN

                                          BCP, p. 715

1 Epiphany ABC

Alleluia III

Al-le - lu - ia, al-le - lu-ia, al-le - lu-ia.

Verse (Gal. 3:27) TONE IIIa

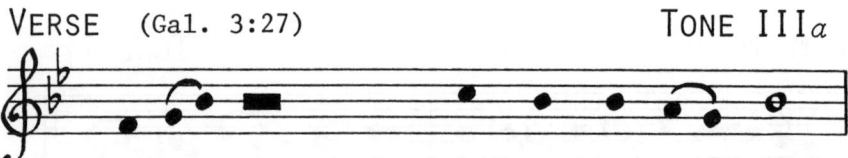

All of you who were bap-tized in - to Christ*

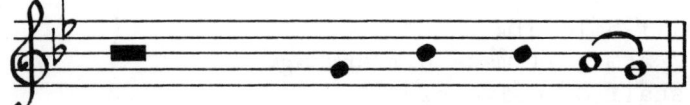

have clothed your-selves with Christ.

Refrain

Pro-claim the glo-ry of the Lord a-mong the na-tions.

Psalm 96   Tone II

1   *Sing to* the LORD a néw song;*
     sing to the LORD, all / the whóle earth.
2   Sing to the LORD and bléss his Name;*
     proclaim the good news of his salvation / from
                    dáy to day.   REFRAIN

3   *De-clare* his glory among the ná-tions*
     and his wonders among / all péo-ples.
4   For great is the LORD and greatly to be praísed;*
     he is more to be feared / than áll gods.

                            REFRAIN

7   *As-cribe* to the LORD, you families of the péo-ples;*
     ascribe to the LORD honor / and pów-er.
8   Ascribe to the LORD the honor due his Náme;*
     bring offerings and come in - / to hís courts.

                            REFRAIN

9   *Wor-ship* the LORD in the beauty of hó-li-ness;*
     let the whole earth tremble / be-fóre him.
10   Tell it out among the nations: "The LÓRD is King!*
     he has made the world so firm that it cannot be moved;
     he will judge the peoples / with éq-ui-ty."

                            REFRAIN

BCP, p. 725

2 Epiphany C

Alleluia IV

Al-le-lu-ia, al-le - lu - ia, al-le - lu-ia.

Verse   (John 2:11)   Tone IVe

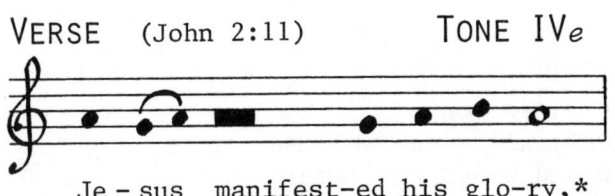

Je - sus   manifest-ed his glo-ry,*

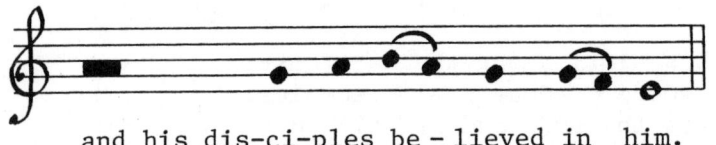

and his dis-ci-ples be - lieved in   him.

3 EPIPHANY C

REFRAIN

From the ris-ing of the sun to its go-ing down

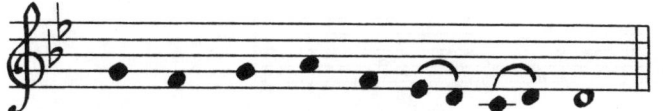

let the Name of the Lord be praised.

PSALM 113   TONE IIIb

1 *Hal - lë - lujah!*
   Give praise, you sér-vants óf thë LORD;*
     praise the Name / of thé LORD.
2 Let the Name of the LÓRD be blëss-ed,*
     from this time forth / for év-er-more.

                               REFRAIN

3 *From thë* rising of the sún to its gó-iṅg down*
     let the Name of / the LÓRD be praised.
4 The LORD is high a-bóve all ñä-tions,*
     and his glory above / the héav-ens.

                               REFRAIN

5 *Who is* like the LORD our God, who síts en-thróned
                       oṅ high,*
     but stoops to behold the heav - / ens añd the earth?
6 He takes up the wéak out óf thë dust*
     and lifts up the poor from / the ásh-es.

                               REFRAIN

(continued)   *BCP, p. 756*

REFRAIN

From the ris-ing of the sun to its go-ing down

let the Name of the Lord be praised.

PSALM 113   TONE IIIb

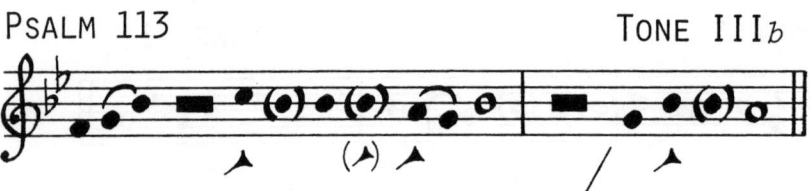

7 *He sets* them wíth the prïn-ces,*
      with the princes of / his péo-ple.
8 He makes the woman óf a chíld-lëss house*
      to be a joyful mother / of chíl-dren.

                                    REFRAIN

3 EPIPHANY C

ALLELUIA VIII

Al-le - lu - ia, al-le-lu - ia, al - le-lu-ia.

VERSE (Luke 4:18,19)   TONE VIIIg

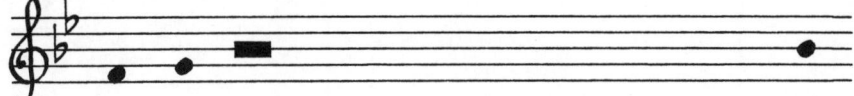

The Lord has anointed me to preach good news to

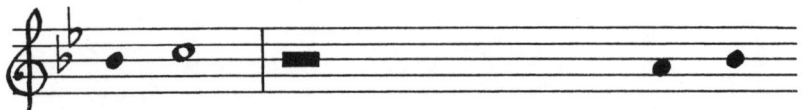

the poor,*   and to set at liberty those who

are op-pressed.

4 EPIPHANY C

REFRAIN

My tongue will pro-claim your right-eous-ness, O God.

PSALM 71   TONE IVe

1 *In you*, O LORD, have I / tak-en réf-uge;*
  let me / nev-er bë ä-shamed.
2 In your righteousness, deliver me and / set me frée;*
  incline your ear / to me aïd säve me.
                                            REFRAIN

3 *Be my* strong rock, a castle to / keep me sáfe;*
  you are my / crag and mÿ strŏng-hold.
4 Deliver me, my God, from the hand / of the wíck-ed,*
  from the clutches of the evildoer / and the
                      öp-pfës-sor.   REFRAIN

5 *For you* are my / hope, O LÓRD God,*
  my con - / fi-dence siñce Í wäs young.
6 I have been sustained by you ever since I was born;
  from my mother's womb you have / been my stréngth;*
  my praise shall / be al-wäys öf you.
                                            REFRAIN

15 *My moüth* shall recount your mighty acts
   and saving deeds / all day lóng;*
   though I cannot know / the num-bër öf them.
17 O God, you have taught me since / I was yoúng,*
   and to this day I tell / of your wön-dér-fül works.
                                            REFRAIN

ALLELUIA - ad libitum

BCP, p. 683

5 Epiphany C

REFRAIN

I will lis-ten to what the Lord God is say-ing.

PSALM 85   TONE Va

7 *Show us* your mercy, O LÓRD,*
   and grant us yóur sal-vá-tion.
8 ·I will listen to what the LORD God is sáy-ing,*
   for he is speaking peace to his faithful people
   and to those who túrn their heárts to him.

                                    REFRAIN

9 *Tru - ly*, his salvation is very near to those
                          who féar him,*
   that his glory may dwéll in oúr land.
10 Mercy and truth have met to-géth-er;*
   righteousness and peace have kis̃sed each óth-er.

                                    REFRAIN

11 *Truth shall* spring up from the eárth,*
   and righteousness shall look dówn from heáv-en.
13 Righteousness shall go be-fóre him,*
   and peace shall be a páth-way fór his feet.

                                    REFRAIN

ALLELUIA - ad libitum

6 EPIPHANY C

REFRAIN

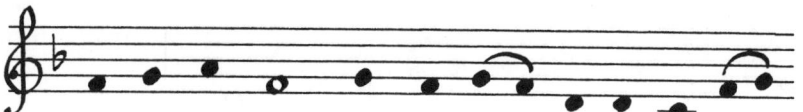

Hap-py are they whose de-light is in the law

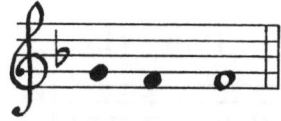

of the Lord.

PSALM 1   TONE VI

1 *Hap - p̈y* are they who have not walked in the counsel
                                    of / the wíck-ed,*
     nor lingered in the way of sinners,
     nor sat in the seats / of thë scórn-ful!
2 Their delight is in the law / of thé LORD,*
     and they meditate on / his läw dáy and night.

                                                        REFRAIN

3 *They är̈e* like trees planted by streams of water,
     bearing fruit in due season, with leaves that
                          do / not wíth-er;*
     everything they / do shäll prós-per.
4 It is not so with / the wíck-ed;*
     they are like chaff which / the wïnd blóws a-way.

                                                        REFRAIN

5 *There - for̈e* the wicked shall not stand upright / when
                          júdg-ment comes,*
     nor the sinner in the council / of thë ríght-eous.
6 For the LORD knows the way of / the ríght-eous,*
     but the way of the / wick-ëd ís doomed.

                                                        REFRAIN

ALLELUIA - ad libitum   *BCP, p. 585*

7 EPIPHANY C

REFRAIN

Put your trust in the Lord and do good.

PSALM 37   TONE VIIb

1 *Do not* fret yourself because of é-vil-dó-ers;*
    do not be jealous of thóse who dó wrong.
3 Put your trust in the LÓRD and dó good;*
    dwell in the land and féed on its rích-es.

                                                    REFRAIN

4 *Take dë - —— light* in thé LORD,*
    and he shall gíve you your heárt's de-sire.
5 Commit your way to the LORD and pút your trúst in him,*
    and he will bríng it tó pass.

                                                    REFRAIN

6 *He will* make your righteousness as cléar as thé light*
    and your just dealing ás the nóon-day.
7 Be stíll be-fóre the LORD*
    and wait pá-tient-lý for him.

                                                    REFRAIN

8 *Do not* fret yourself over the one who prós-pers,*
    the one who suc-céeds in é-vil schemes.
10 For evildoers shall be cút off,*
    but those who wait upon the LORD shall pos-séss
                        the land.

                                                    REFRAIN

ALLELUIA - ad libitum

8 EPIPHANY C

REFRAIN

It is a good thing to give thanks to the Lord.

PSALM 92   TONE VIII*g*

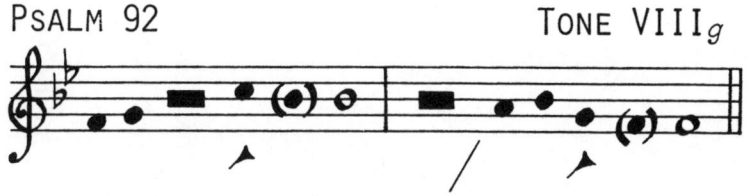

2 *To tell* of your loving-kindness early in the mórn-ing*
     and of your faithfulness in / the night séa-son;
3 On the psaltery, and on the lýre,*
     and to the mel - / o-dy óf the harp.

REFRAIN

11 *The right* - eous shall flourish like a pálm tree,*
      and shall spread abroad like a ce - / dar of Lé-ba-non.
12 Those who are planted in the house of the LÓRD*
      shall flourish in the / courts of oúr God;

REFRAIN

13 *They shall* still bear fruit in óld age;*
      they shall be / green and súc-cu-lent;
14 That they may show how upright the LÓRD is,*
      my Rock, in / whom there iś no fault.

REFRAIN

ALLELUIA - ad libitum

REFRAIN

Pro-claim the great-ness of the Lord our God;

he is the Ho - ly One.

PSALM 99   TONE VIII*g*

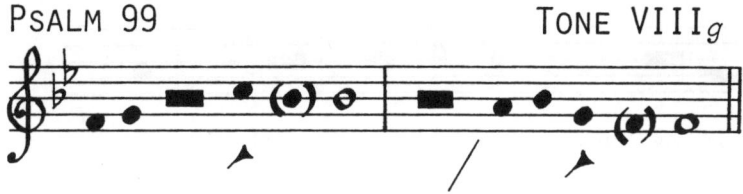

1   *The LORD* is King;
    let the people trém-ble;*
        he is enthroned upon the cherubim;
        / let the eárth shake.
2   The LORD is great in Zí-on;*
        he is high a - / bove all péo-ples.

                                    REFRAIN

6   *Mo - ses* and Aaron among his priests,
    and Samuel among those who call up-ón his Name,*
        they called upon the LORD, / and he án-swered them.
7   He spoke to them out of the pillar of cloúd;*
        they kept his testimonies and the decree / that
                        he gáve them.

                                    REFRAIN

8   *O LORD* our God, you answered thém in-deed;*
        you were a God who forgave them,
        yet punished them / for their é-vil deeds.
9   Proclaim the greatness of the LORD our God
    and worship him upon his hó-ly hill;*
        for the LORD our God / is the Hó-ly One.

                                    REFRAIN

                                    BCP, p. 728

LAST EPIPHANY C

ALLELUIA VIII

Al-le - lu - ia, al-le-lu - ia, al - le-lu-ia.

VERSE (Matt. 17:5)   TONE VIIIg

This is my Son, my Be-lov-ed,* with whom I am

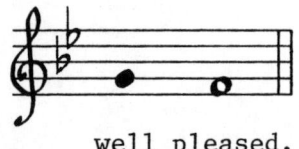

well pleased.

ASH WEDNESDAY ABC

REFRAIN

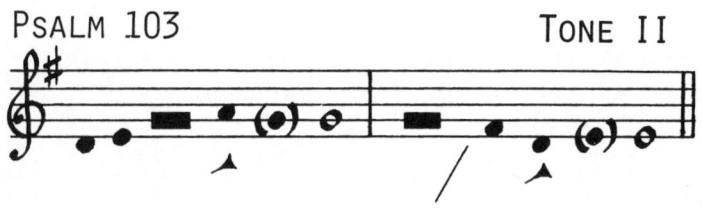

The Lord re-mem-bers that we are but dust.

PSALM 103   TONE II

8 *The LORD* is full of compassion and mér-cy,*
      slow to anger and of / great kińd-ness.
9 He will not always ac-cúse us,*
      nor will he keep his anger / for év-er.

                              REFRAIN

10 *He has* not dealt with us according to our síns,*
      nor rewarded us according to / our wíck-ed-ness.
11 For as the heavens are high above the eárth,*
      so is his mercy great upon those / who feár him.

                              REFRAIN

12 *As far* as the east is from the wést,*
      so far has he removed / our síns from us.
13 As a father cares for his chíl-dren,*
      so does the LORD care for those / who feár him.

                              REFRAIN

TONE II

VERSE (2 Cor. 6:2)

Be - hold, now is the acceptable tíme;*
   behold, now is the day of / sal-vá-tion.

OR

TRACT (Psalm 130)

1 *Out of* the depths have I called to you, O LORD;
   LORD, héar my voice;*
      let your ears consider well the voice
                     of my sup - / pli-cá-tion.

2 If you, LORD, were to note what is dóne a-miss,*
   O Lord, / who cóuld stand?

3 For there is forgiveness with yóu;*
   therefore / you sháll be feared.

4 I wait for the LORD; my soul wáits for him;*
   in his word / is mý hope.

5 My soul waits for the LORD,
   more than watchmen for the mórn-ing,*
      more than watchmen for / the mórn-ing.

6 O Israel, wait for the LÓRD,*
   for with the LORD there / is mér-cy;

7 With him there is plenteous re-démp-tion,*
   and he shall redeem Israel / from áll their sins.

1 Lent C

Refrain

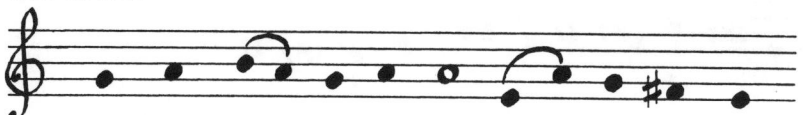

He shall give his an-gels charge o - ver you,

to keep you in all your ways.

Psalm 91   Tone IVa

9 *Be - caüse* you have made the / LORD your réf-uge,*
     and the Most High / your hab-i-tá-tion,
10 There shall no evil / hap-pen tó you,*
     neither shall any plague / come near your dwéll-ing.

                                                    REFRAIN

12 *They shäll* bear you / in their hánds,*
     lest you dash / your foot a-gáinst a stone.
13 You shall tread upon the li - / on and ád-der;*
     you shall trample the young lion and the ser - / pent
            un-der yóur feet.

                                                    REFRAIN

14 *Be - caüse* he is bound to me in love,
     therefore will / I de-lív-er him;*
     I will protect him, / be-cause he knóws my Name.
15 He shall call upon me, and / I will án-swer him;*
     I am with him in trouble;
     I will rescue him and / bring him to hón-or.

                                                    REFRAIN

1 LENT C

TONE II

VERSE (Matt. 4:4)

Man shall not live by bréad a-lone,*
   but by every word that proceeds from / the móuth
      of God.

OR

TRACT (Psalm 91)

1 *He who* dwells in the shelter of the Móst High,*
      abides under the shadow of the / Al-míght-y.

2 He shall say to the LORD,
   "You are my refuge and my stróng-hold,*
      my God in whom / I pút my trust."

3 He shall deliver you from the snare of the húnt-er*
      and from the dead - / ly pés-ti-lence.

4 He shall cover you with his pinions,
   and you shall find refuge under his wíngs;*
      his faithfulness shall be a shield / and búck-ler.

11 For he shall give his angels charge ó-ver you,*
      to keep you / in áll your ways.

12 They shall bear you in their hánds,*
      lest you dash your foot / a-gáinst a stone.

REFRAIN

The Lord is my light and my sal - va - tion.

PSALM 27   TONE IV*e*

10 *Heark - ën* to my voice, O LORD, / when I cáll;*
 have mercy / on me aṅd áṅ-swër me.
11 You speak in my heart / and say, "Séek my face."*
 Your / face, LORD, will Ï seek.

           REFRAIN

12 *Hide nöt* your / face from mé,*
 nor turn away your ser - / vant in dïs-pléäs-ure.
13 You have been my helper;
 cast me / not a-wáy;*
  do not forsake me, O God / of my säl-väi-tion.

           REFRAIN

14 *Though mÿ* father and my moth - / er for-sáke me,*
 the / LORD will süs-taïn me.
15 Show / me your wáy, O LORD;*
 lead me on a level path, be - / cause of mÿ éṅ-ë-mies.

           REFRAIN

17 *What ïf* I had not believed
 that I should see the goodness / of the LÓRD*
 in the / land of thë lïv-ing!
18 O tarry and await the LORD'S pleasure;
 be strong, and he shall / com-fort yóur heart;*
 wait / pa-tient-lÿ fór thë LORD.

           REFRAIN

2 LENT C

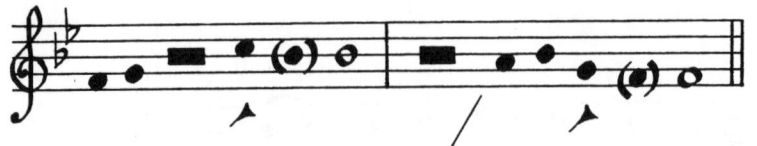

VERSE (Amos 5:14)

Seek good, and not evil, that yóu may live;*
and the God of hosts / will be wíth you.

OR

TRACT (Psalm 106)

1 *Give thanks* to the LORD, for hé is good,*
for his mercy en - / dures for év-er.

2 Who can declare the mighty acts of the LÓRD*
or / show forth áll his praise?

3 Happy are those who act with jús-tice*
and always / do what ís right!

4 Remember me, O LORD, with the favor you have
for your péo-ple,*
and visit me / with your sáv-ing help;

5 That I may see the prosperity of your elect
and be glad with the gladness of your péo-ple,*
that I may glory with / your in-hér-i-tance.

2 LENT C *(alternate)*

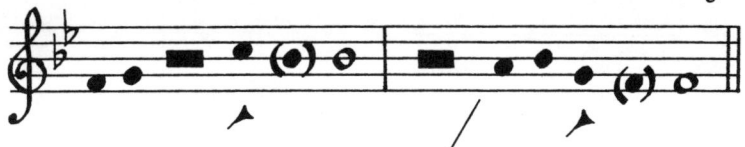

VERSE (Amos 5:14)

Seek good, and not evil, that yóu may live;*
and the God of hosts / will be wíth you.

OR

TRACT (Psalm 25:16-21)

16 *The sor* - rows of my heart háve in-creased;*
bring me out / of my tróub-les.

17 Look upon my adversity and mís-er-y*
and for - / give me áll my sin.

18 Look upon my enemies, for they are mán-y,*
and they bear a violent ha - / tred a-gáinst me.

19 Protect my life and de-lív-er me;*
let me not be put to shame, for I have / trust-ed
ín you.

20 Let integrity and uprightness pre-sérve me,*
for my / hope has beén in you.

21 Deliver Israel, O Gód,*
out of / all his tróub-les.

3 LENT C

REFRAIN

The Lord is full of com-pas-sion and mer-cy,

slow to an-ger and of great kind-ness.

PSALM 103   TONE IVa

1 *Bless the* LORD, / O my soul,*
   and all that is within / me, bless his ho-ly Name.
2 Bless the LORD, / O my soul,*
   and forget / not all his ben-e-fits.

                        REFRAIN

3 *He for* - gives / all your sins*
   and heals / all your in-fir-mi-ties;
4 He redeems your life / from the grave*
   and crowns you with mercy / and lov-ing-kind-ness;

                        REFRAIN

6 *The LORD* ex - / e-cutes right-eous-ness*
   and judgment / for all who are op-pressed.
7 He made his ways / known to Mo-ses*
   and his works to the / chil-dren of Is-ra-el.

                        REFRAIN

10 *He has* not dealt with us according / to our sins,*
    nor rewarded us accord - / ing to our wick-ed-ness.
11 For as the heavens are / high a-bove the earth,*
    so is his mercy great up - / on those who fear him.

                        REFRAIN

BCP, p. 733

3 Lent C

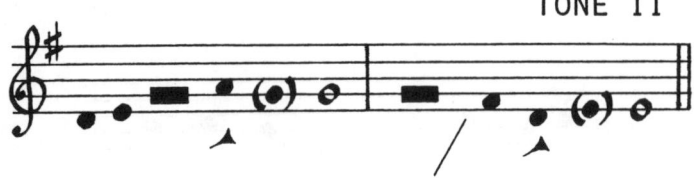

Verse (2 Cor. 6:2)

Be - *hold*, now is the acceptable tíme;*
behold, now is the day of / sal-vá-tion.

Tract (Psalm 42:1-7)

1 *As the* deer longs for the wá-ter-brooks,*
   so longs my soul / for yóu, O God.

2 My soul is athirst for God, athirst for the
                          lív-ing God;*
   when shall I come to appear before the
                          pres - / ence óf God?

3 My tears have been my food dáy and night,*
   while all day long they say to me,
   "Where / now iś your God?"

4 I pour out my soul when I think on thése things:*
   how I went with the multitude and led them
                          into / the hóuse of God,

5 With the voice of praise and thánks-giv-ing,*
   among those who / keep hó-ly-day.

6 Why are you so full of heaviness, Ó my soul?*
   and why are you so disquieted / with-ín me?

7 Put your trúst in God;*
   for I will yet give thanks to him,
   who is the help of my counte - / nance, añd my God.

4 Lent C

REFRAIN

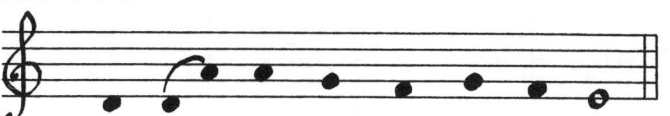

Taste and see that the Lord is good.

PSALM 34

TONE IVe

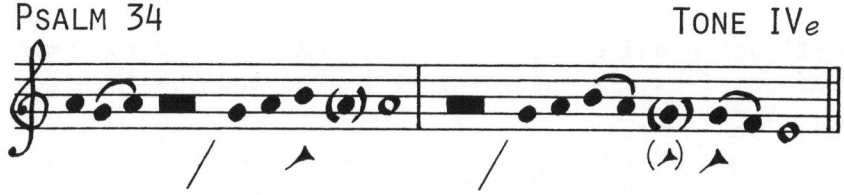

1 *I will* bless the / LORD at áll times;*
   his praise shall / ev-er bë ín mÿ mouth.
2 I will glory / in the LÓRD;*
   let the / hum-ble hëar añd rë-joice.

REFRAIN

3 *Pro - claim* with me the greatness / of the LÓRD;*
   let us exalt / his Name tö-gëth-er.
4 I sought the LORD, / and he án-swered me*
   and delivered me out / of all mÿ tër-ror.

REFRAIN

5 *Look up* - on him / and be rá-di-ant,*
   and let not your / fa-ces bë ä-shamed.
6 I called in my affliction and / the LORD heárd me*
   and saved me / from all mÿ tróub-les.

REFRAIN

7 *The än* - gel of the LORD encompasses / those
                    who feár him,*
   and / he will dë-lív-er them.
8 Taste and see / that the LÓRD is good;*
   happy / are they whö trúst iñ him!

REFRAIN

BCP, p. 627

4 LENT C

TONE II

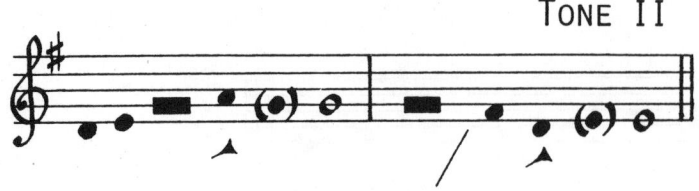

VERSE (Luke 15:18)

I *will* arise and go to my Father, and will sáy to him:*
Father, I have sinned against heaven and / be-fóre you.

OR

TRACT (Psalm 122)

1 I *was* glad when they sáid to me,*
    "Let us go to the house / of thé LORD."

2 Now our feet are stánd-ing*
    within your gates, O / Je-rú-sa-lem.

3 Jerusalem is built as a cít-y*
    that is at uni - / ty wíth it-self.

4 To which the tribes go up,
    the tribes of the LÓRD,*
      the assembly of Israel,
      to praise the Name / of thé LORD.

5 For there are the thrones of júdg-ment,*
    the thrones of the house / of Dá-vid.

6 Pray for the peace of Je-rú-sa-lem:*
    "May they prosper / who lóve you.

7 Peace be within your wálls*
    and quietness within / your tów-ers.

8 For my brethren and com-pán-ions' sake,*
    I pray for your / pros-pér-i-ty.

9 Because of the house of the LÓRD our God,*
    I will seek / to dó you good."

REFRAIN

The Lord has done great things for us,

and we are glad in - deed.

PSALM 126   TONE IV*e*

/   ⟋   /   (⟋) ⟋

1 *When the* LORD restored the for - / tunes of Zí-on,*
    then / were we likë thóse whö dream.
2 Then was our mouth / filled with laúgh-ter,*
    and / our tongue wïth shóuts öf joy.
                                          REFRAIN

3 *Then they* said a - / mong the ná-tions,*
    "The LORD / has done grëat thiñgs för them."
4 The LORD has / done great thiñgs for us,*
    —— / and we ar̈e glád iñ-deed.
                                          REFRAIN

5 *Re - store* our for - / tunes, O LÓRD,*
    like the watercour - / ses of thë N̈e-gev.
6 Those who / sowed with teárs*
    will / reap with soñgs öf joy.
                                          REFRAIN

7 *Those who* go out weeping, carry - / ing the séed,*
    will come again with joy, / shoul-der-iñg
                their sheaves.
                                          REFRAIN

BCP, p. 782

5 LENT C

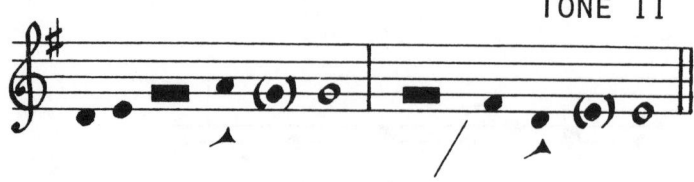

VERSE   (Psalm 118:22-23)

The stone which the builders rejected
has become the chief cór-ner-stone;*
    this is the Lord's doing, and it is
                    marvelous / in oúr eyes.

OR

TRACT   (Psalm 129)

1 *"Great - ly* have they oppressed me siñce my youth,"*
    let Is - / ra-él now say;

2 "Greatly have they oppressed me siñce my youth,*
    but they have not prevailed / a-gáinst me."

3 The plowmen plowed up-ón my back*
    and made / their fúr-rows long.

4 The LORD, the Ríght-eous One,*
    has cut the cords of / the wíck-ed.

5 Let them be put to shame and thrówn back,*
    all those who are enemies / of Zí-on.

6 Let them be like grass upon the hoúse-tops,*
    which withers before / it cán be plucked;

7 Which does not fill the hand of the réap-er,*
    nor the bosom of him / who bínds the sheaves;

8 So that those who go by say not so much as,
    "The LORD prós-per you.*
        We wish you well in the Name / of thé LORD."

During the procession, all hold branches in their hands and appropriate hymns, psalms, or anthems are sung, such as the hymn "All glory, laud and honor," and the following Psalm:

ANTIPHON

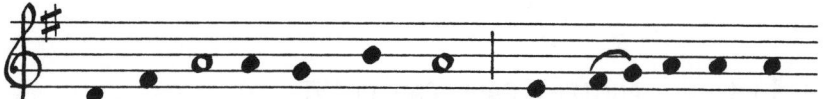

Ho-san-na in the high-est. Bless-ed is he who

comes in the name of the Lord.

(REFRAIN)

*Ho-san-na in the high-est.**

(* The italicized portion of the Anti-phon is to be repeated as a Refrain after each verse of the Psalm.)

PSALM 118   ANCIENT GALLICAN CHANT

19 *O - pen* for me the gates of righteousness;*
     I will enter them;
     I will offer thanks to / the LÓRD.   *Refrain*

20 *This is* the gate of the LORD;*
     he who is righteous / may én-ter."   *Refrain*

REFRAIN

Ho-san-na in the high-est.

PSALM 118   ANCIENT GALLICAN CHANT

21 *I will* give thanks to you, for you answered me*
    and have become my / sal-vá-tion.   *Refrain*

22 *The same* stone which the builders rejected*
    has become the / chief cór-ner-stone.   *Refrain*

23 *This is* the LORD'S doing,*
    and it is marve - / lous ín in our eyes.   *Refrain*

24 *On this* day the LORD has acted;*
    we will rejoice and / be glád in it.   *Refrain*

25 *Ho - san* - nah, LORD, hosannah!*
    LORD, send / us nów suc-cess.   *Refrain*

26 *Bless - ed* is he who comes in the name of the Lord;*
    we bless you from the house of / the LÖRD.
                                                 Refrain

27 *God is* the LORD; he has shined upon us;*
    form a procession with branches up to
                    the horns of / the ál-tar.
                                                 Refrain

(continued)

REFRAIN

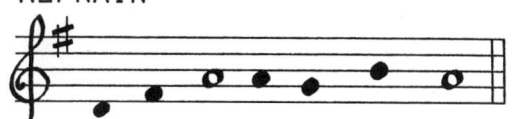

Ho-san-na in the high-est.

PSALM 118   ANCIENT GALLICAN CHANT

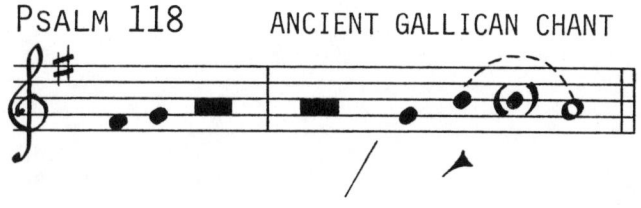

28 *"You are* my God, and I will thank you;*
      you are my God, and I will / ex-ált you."

                                                    Refrain

29 *Give thanks* to the LORD, for he is good;*
      his mercy endures / for év-er.   *Refrain*

THE COMPLETE ANTIPHON
MAY THEN BE REPEATED.

═══════

This Psalm is taken from *Music for Ministers and Congregation* (The Church Hymnal Corporation, ©1978), and is used by permission in this Psalm Collection. Additional music for the Sunday of the Passion can be found in *Music for Ministers and Congregation*, pages 28-31.

PASSION (PALM) SUNDAY C

At the Procession:

REFRAIN

Ho - san - na in the high-est.

PSALM 118   TONE VIIa

19 Ö - *pën* for me the gátes of ríght-eous-ness;*
    I will enter them;
    I will offer thánks to thé LORD.
                                                    REFRAIN

20 "*Thïs ïs* the gáte of thé LORD;*
    he who is ríght-eous may én-tër."
                                                    REFRAIN

21 *I wïll* give thanks to you, fór you án-swered me*
    and have be-cóme my sal-vá-tïön.
                                                    REFRAIN

22 *The same* stone which the búild-ers re-jéct-ed*
    has be-cóme the chief cór-ner-stöne.
                                                    REFRAIN

23 —— This ís the LORD'S dó-ing,*
    and it is már-vel-ous ín our eÿes.
                                                    REFRAIN

24 *Ön thïs* day the LÓRD has áct-ed;*
    we will re-jóice and be glád in ït.
                                                    REFRAIN

(continued)

PASSION (PALM) SUNDAY C *(continuation)*

At the Procession:

REFRAIN

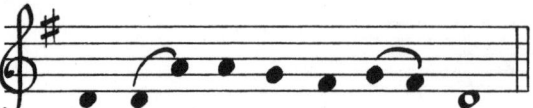

Ho - san - na in the high-est.

PSALM 118   TONE VIIa

25 *Ho - san* - nah, LÓRD, ho-sán-nah!*
    LORD, sénd us nów suc-cëss.

REFRAIN

26 *Blëss - ëd* is he who comes in the náme of thé Lord;*
    we bless you from the hóuse of thé LÖRD.

REFRAIN

27 *God is* the LORD; he has shíned up-ón us;*
    form a procession with branches up to the
                        hórns of the ál-tär.

REFRAIN

28 *"You are* my God, and Í will thánk you;*
    you are my God, and Í will ex-ált yöu."

REFRAIN

29 *Give thanks* to the LÓRD, for hé is good;*
    his mercy en-dúres for év-ër.

REFRAIN

BCP, p. 762

PASSION (PALM) SUNDAY C

At the Eucharist:

REFRAIN

My God, my God, why have you for - sak-en me?

PSALM 22   TONE IV*e*

1 *My God*, my God, why have / you for-sák-en me?*
      and are so far from my cry
      and from / the words öf mý dïs-tress?
2 O my God, I cry in the daytime, but you / do
                              not án-swer;*
      by night as well, / but I fïnd nö̈ rest.
3 Yet you / are the Hó-ly One,*
      enthroned upon the / prais-es öf Iś-ra̤-el.

                                    REFRAIN

4 *Our fore* - fathers / put their trúst in you;*
      they trusted, / and you dë-lív-ered them.
5 They cried out to you and / were de-lív-ered;*
      they trusted in you / and were nöt pút tö shame.
6 But as for me, I am a / worm and nó man,*
      scorned by all and de - / spised by thë pëö-ple.

                                    REFRAIN

7 *All who* see me laugh / me to scórn;*
      they curl their lips and / wag their heads, sa̤y-ing,*
8 "He trusted in the LORD; let / him de-lív-er him;*
      let him rescue him, / if he dë-líghts in̈ him."
9 Yet you are he who took me out / of the wómb,*
      and kept me safe / up-on mÿ móth-ër's breast.

                                    REFRAIN

(continued)

BCP, p. 610

At the Eucharist

REFRAIN

My   God, my God, why have you for - sak-en me?

PSALM 22   TONE IV*e*

10 *I have* been entrusted to you ev - / er since Í was born;*
    you were my God when I was / still in mÿ
                      móth-ër's womb.
11 Be not far from me, for trou - / ble is néar,*
    ── / and there iš nóne tö help.
                                            REFRAIN

Passion (Palm) Sunday C

Tone II

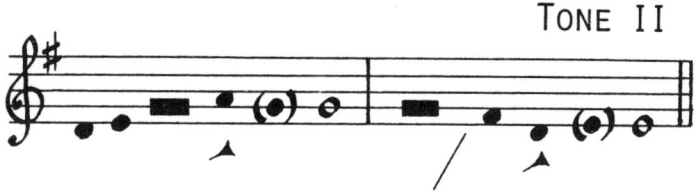

Verse (Phil. 2:8,9)

Christ for us became obedient unto death, even
death on a cróss;*
therefore God has highly exalted him
and bestowed on him the name which is a - / bove
eve-ry name.

OR

Tract (Psalm 22)

26 *All the* ends of the earth shall remember and turn to
the LÓRD,*
and all the families of the nations shall
bow / be-fóre him.

27 For kingship belongs to the LÓRD;*
he rules over / the ná-tions.

28 To him alone all who sleep in the earth bow down
in wór-ship;*
all who go down to the dust fall / be-fóre him.

29 My soul shall live for him;
my descendants shall sérve him;*
they shall be known as the LORD'S / for év-er.

30 They shall come and make known to a people yét un-born*
the saving deeds / that hé has done.

REFRAIN

In your light, O God, we see light.

PSALM 36   TONE I*g*

5 *Your love*, O LORD, reaches tó the héav-ens,*
    and your faith - / ful-ness tö the clouds.
6 Your righteousness is like the strong mountains,
    your justice líke the gréat deep;*
    you save both / man and béäst, O LORD.

                                     REFRAIN

7 *How price* - less ís your lóve, O God!*
    your people take refuge under the
                    sha - / dow of yöür wings.
8 They feast upon the a-bún-dance óf your house;*
    you give them drink from the ri - / ver of
            yöür de-lights.

                                     REFRAIN

9 *For with* you ís the wéll of life,*
    and in your / light we séë light.
10 Continue your loving-kindness to thóse who knów you,*
    and your favor to those / who are trüe of heart.

                                     REFRAIN

Monday in Holy Week ABC

Tone II

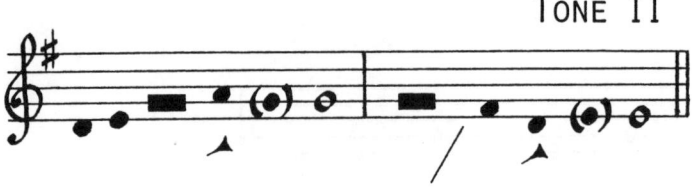

Verse

We a - dore you, O Christ, and we bléss you,*
    because by your holy cross you have / re-deémed
        the world.

OR

Tract   (Psalm 102)

1 *LORD, hear* my prayer, and let my cry come be-fóre you;*
    hide not your face from me in the day of / my tróu-ble.

2 Incline your eár to me;*
    when I call, make haste / to án-swer me.

3 For my days drift away like smóke,*
    and my bones are hot / as búrn-ing coals.

4 My heart is smitten like grass and wíth-ered,*
    so that I forget / to eát my bread.

12 But you, O LORD, endure for év-er,*
    and your Name / from áge to age.

13 You will arise and have compassion on Zion,
    for it is time to have mercy up-ón her;*
    indeed, the appoint - / ed tíme has come.

REFRAIN

I have tak-en ref-uge in you, O Lord.

PSALM 71   TONE II

2   *In your* righteousness, deliver me and sét me free;*
    incline your ear to me / and sáve me.
3   Be my strong rock, a castle to kéep me safe;*
    you are my crag and / my stróng-hold.
                                        REFRAIN

4   *De - liv -* er me, my God, from the hand of the wíck-ed,*
    from the clutches of the evildoer and
                        the / op-prés-sor.
10 For my enemies are talking a-gaínst me,*
    and those who lie in wait for my life take
                        counsel / to-géth-er.
                                        REFRAIN

11 *They say,* "God has forsaken him;
    go after him and séize him;*
    because there is none / who wíll save."
12 O God, be not fár from me;*
    come quickly to help / me, Ó my God.
                                        REFRAIN

VERSE OR TRACT AS ON MONDAY

REFRAIN

An-swer me, O God, in your great mer-cy.

PSALM 69   TONE IIIa

7 *Let not* those who hope in you be put to shame through mé,
  Lord GOD öf hosts;*
    let not those who seek you be disgraced because of me,
      O God / of Iś-ra-ël.
8 Surely, for your sake have I súf-fered fë-proach,*
    and shame has cov - / ered mý fáce.

REFRAIN

9 *I have* become a stranger to mý own kín-dred,*
    an alien to my moth - / er's chíl-drën.
10 Zeal for your house has eát-en më up;*
    the scorn of those who scorn you has fallen / up-ón më.

REFRAIN

14 *But as* for me, thís is my práyer tö you,*
    at the time you / have sét, O LÓRD:
15 "In your great mér-cy, Ö God,*
    answer me with your / un-fáil-ing hëlp."

REFRAIN

22 *Re - proach* has broken my heart, and it cán-not
      bë healed;*
    I looked for sympathy, but there was none,
    for comforters, but I could / find nó ońe.
23 They gáve me gáll tö eat,*
    and when I was thirsty, they gave me vine - / gar tó
      drïnk.

REFRAIN

VERSE OR TRACT AS ON MONDAY

BCP, p. 679

Maundy Thursday ABC

Refrain

Mor-tals ate the bread of an-gels,

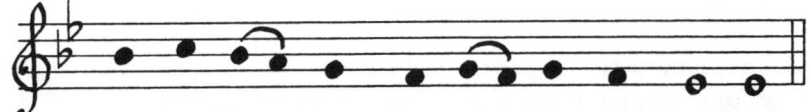

for the Lord gave them man-na from heav-en.

Psalm 78   Tone Va

14 *He led* them with a cloud by day,*
    and all the night through with a glow of fire.
15 He split the hard rocks in the wil-der-ness*
    and gave them drink as from the great deep.

REFRAIN

17 *But they* went on sinning a-gainst him,*
    rebelling in the desert a-gainst the Most High.
18 They tested God in their hearts,*
    demanding food for their crav-ing.

REFRAIN

19 *They railed* against God and said,*
    "Can God set a table in the wil-der-ness?"
23 So he commanded the clouds a-bove*
    and opened the doors of heav-en.

REFRAIN

24 *He rained* down manna upon them to eat*
    and gave them grain from heav-en.
25 So mortals ate the bread of an-gels;*
    he provided for them food e-nough.   REFRAIN

BCP, p. 696

Maundy Thursday ABC

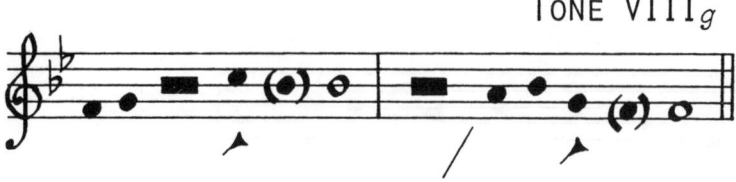

Verse   (John 13:34)

A *new* commandment I gíve to you:*
love one another as / I have lóved you.

OR

Tract   (Psalm 43)

1 *Give judg* - ment for me, O God,
   and defend my cause against an ungodly péo-ple;*
      deliver me from the deceitful / and the ẃick-ed.

2 For you are the God of my strength;
   why have you put me fróm you?*
      and why do I go so heavily while the ene - / my
                     op-préss-es me?

3 Send out your light and your truth, that they
                     may leád me,*
      and bring me to your holy hill
      and / to your dwéll-ing;

4 That I may go to the altar of God,
   to the God of my joy and glád-ness;*
      and on the harp I will give thanks to / you,
                     O Gód my God.

5 Why are you so full of heaviness, Ó my soul?*
      and why are you so disquiet - / ed with-ín me?

6 Put your trúst in God;*
      for I will yet give thanks to him,
      who is the help of my coun - / te-nance, ánd my God.

GOOD FRIDAY ABC

REFRAIN

My God, my God, why have you for-sak-en me?

PSALM 22   TONE IVe

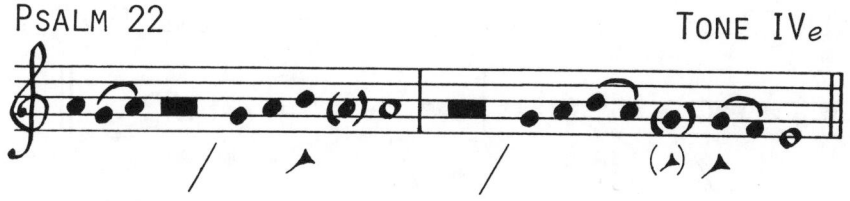

1 *My God*, my God, why have / you for-sák-en me?*
      and are so far from my cry
      and from / the words öf mý dïs-tress?
2 O my God, I cry in the daytime, but you / do not
                              án-swer;*
      by night as well, / but I find nö rest.

                                        REFRAIN

7 *All who* see me laugh / me to scórn;*
      they curl their lips and / wag their heäds, säy-ing,
8 "He trusted in the LORD; let / him de-lív-er him;*
      let him rescue him, / if he dë-líghts in him."

                                        REFRAIN

14 *I am* poured out like water;
      all my / bones are oút of joint;*
      my heart within / my breast ïs mélt-ïng wax.
15 My mouth is dried out like a pot-sherd;
      my tongue sticks to the roof / of my moúth;*
      and you have laid me / in the düst óf thë grave.

                                        REFRAIN

(continued)

REFRAIN

My God, my God, why have you for-sak-en me?

PSALM 22   TONE IV*e*

16 *Packs öf* dogs close me in,
    and gangs of evildoers cir - / cle a-roúnd me;*
       they pierce my hands and my feet;
       / I can coünt áll mÿ bones.
17 They stare and gloat / o-ver mé;*
       they divide my garments among them;
       they cast / lots for mÿ cloth-ing.
                                          REFRAIN

18 *Be nöt* —— / far a-wáy, O LORD;*
       you are my strength; / has-ten tö help me.
19 Save me / from the swórd,*
       my life from / the pow-ër óf thë dog.
                                          REFRAIN

20 *Save mè* —— / from the lí-on's mouth,*
       my wretched body / from the hörns óf wïld bulls.
21 I will declare your Name / to my bréth-ren;*
       in the midst of the congrega - / tion I wïll
                      práïse you.
                                          REFRAIN

GOOD FRIDAY ABC

TONE II

VERSE (Phil. 2:8,9)

> *Christ for* us became obedient unto death,
> even death on a cróss;*
>> therefore God has highly exalted him
>> and bestowed on him the name which is a - / bove
>>> eve-ry name.

OR

TRACT (Psalm 40)

1 *I wait* - ed patiently up-ón the LORD;*
   he stooped to me / and heárd my cry.

2 He lifted me out of the desolate pit,
                  out of the míre and clay;*
      he set my feet upon a high cliff
                  and made / my fóot-ing sure.

3 He put a new song in my mouth,
   a song of praise to our Gód;*
      many shall see, and stand in awe,
      and put their trust / in thé LORD.

4 Happy are they who trust in the LÓRD!*
      they do not resort to evil spirits
                  or turn / to fálse gods.

5 Great things are they that you have done, O LORD my God!
   how great your wonders and your pláns for us!*
      there is none who can be / com-páred with you.

6 Oh, that I could make them known and téll them!*
      but they are more / than Í can count.

(continued)

TONE II

7   In sacrifice and offering you take no pléas-ure*
    (you have given me ears / to héar you);

8   Burnt-offering and sin-offering you have nót re-quired,*
    and so I said, / "Be-hóld, I come.

9   In the roll of the book it is written con-cérn-ing me:*

    'I love to do your will, O my God;
    your law is deep / in mý heart.'"

10 I proclaimed righteousness in the great con-gre-gá-tion;*
    behold, I did not restrain my lips;
    and that, / O LÓRD, you know.

11 Your righteousness have I not hidden in my heart;
    I have spoken of your faithfulness and your
                        de-lív-er-ance;*
    I have not concealed your love and faithfulness
                        from the great con - / gre-gá-tion.

12 You are the LORD;
    do not withhold your compassion fróm me;*
    let your love and your faithfulness keep
                        me safe / for év-er,

13 For innumerable troubles have crowded upon me;
    my sins have overtaken me, and I cán-not see;*
        they are more in number than the hairs of my head,
    and my / heart fáils me.

14 Be pleased, O LORD, to de-lív-er me;*
    O LORD, make haste / to hélp me.

GOOD FRIDAY ABC

VERSE (Phil. 2:8,9)

Christ for us became obedient unto death,
even death on a cróss;*
    therefore God has highly exalted him
    and bestowed on him the name which is a - / bove
           éve-ry name.

OR

TRACT (Psalm 69)

1 —— Save me, O Gód,*
    for the waters have risen up / to mý neck.

2 I am sinking in deép mire,*
    and there is no firm ground / for mý feet.

3 I have come into deep wá-ters,*
    and the torrent wash - / es ó-ver me.

4 I have grown weary with my crying;
  my throat is in-flámed;*
    my eyes have failed from look - / ing fór my God.

5 Those who hate me without a cause are more than
           the hairs of my head;
  my lying foes who would destroy me are míght-y.*
  Must I then give back what / I név-er stole?

6 O God, you know my foól-ish-ness,*
    and my faults are not hid - / den fróm you.

7 Let not those who hope in you be put to shame through me,
           Lord GÓD of hosts;*
  let not those who seek you be disgraced because of me,
           O God / of Ís-ra-el.

(continued)

TONE II

8   Surely, for your sake have I suffered re-próach,*
    and shame has cov - / ered mý face.

9   I have become a stranger to my own kín-dred,*
    an alien to my moth - / er's chíl-dren.

10 Zeal for your house has eaten me úp;*
    the scorn of those who scorn you has fallen / up-ón me.

14 But as for me, this is my práyer to you,*
    at the time you / have sét, O LORD:

15 "In your great mercy, O Gód,*
    answer me with your / un-fáil-ing help.

16 Save me from the mire; do not let me sínk;*
    let me be rescued from those who hate me
    and out of the / deep wá-ters.

17 Let not the torrent of waters wash over me,
    neither let the deep swallow me úp;*
    do not let the Pit shut its mouth / up-ón me.

18 Answer me, O LORD, for your lóve is kind;*
    in your great compas - / sion, túrn to me."

19 "Hide not your face from your sér-vant;*
    be swift and answer me, for I / am ín dis-tress.

20 Draw near to me and re-deém me;*
    because of my enemies / de-lív-er me.

21 You know my reproach, my shame, and my dis-hón-or;*
    my adversaries are all / in yóur sight."

(continued)

TONE II

22 Reproach has broken my heart, and it cannot be héaled;*
      I looked for sympathy, but there was none,
      for comforters, but I could / find nó one.

23 They gave me gáll to eat,*
      and when I was thirsty, they gave me vin - / e-gár
                          to drink.

Holy Saturday ABC

Refrain

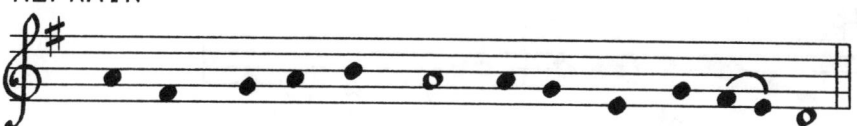

Fa-ther, in-to your hands I com-mend my spir-it.

Psalm 31   Tone VIIb

1 *In you,* O LORD, have I taken refuge;
   let me név-er be pút to shame;*
     deliver me ín your ríght-eous-ness.
2 In-clíne your eár to me;*
   make háste to de-lív-er me.

REFRAIN

3 *Be my* strong rock, a castle to keep me safe,
   for you are my crág and my stróng-hold;*
     for the sake of your Name, leád me and gúide me.
4 Take me out of the net that they have sé-cret-ly
               sét for me,*
   for you are my tów-er óf strength.

REFRAIN

5 *In - to* your hands I com-ménd my spír-it,*
   for you have redeemed me,
   O LÓRD, O Gód of truth.
16 Make your face to shine up-ón your sér-vant,*
   and in your loving-kínd-ness sáve me.

REFRAIN

HOLY SATURDAY ABC

TONE II

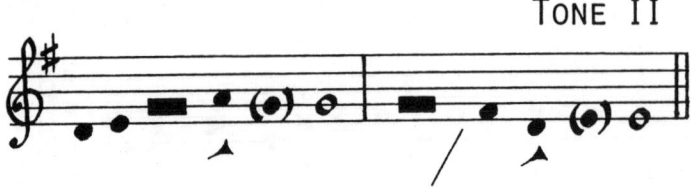

VERSE

*We a-*dore you, O Christ, and we bléss you,*
because by your holy cross you have / re-deémed
the world.

OR

TRACT (Psalm 130)

1 *Out of* the depths have I called to you, O LORD;
LORD, heár my voice;*
let your ears consider well the voice of
my sup - / pli-cá-tion.

2 If you, LORD, were to note what is dóne a-miss,*
O Lord, / who coúld stand?

3 For there is forgiveness with yóu;*
therefore / you sháll be feared.

4 I wait for the LORD; my soul wáits for him;*
in his word / is mý hope.

5 My soul waits for the LORD,
more than watchmen for the mórn-ing,*
more than watchmen for / the mórn-ing.

6 O Israel, wait for the LÓRD,*
for with the LORD there / is mér-cy.

7 With him there is plenteous re-démp-tion,*
and he shall redeem Israel / from áll their sins.

EASTER VIGIL ABC

REFRAIN

By the word of the Lord were the heav-ens made,

by the breath of his mouth all the heav-en-ly hosts.

PSALM 33

TONE I*f*

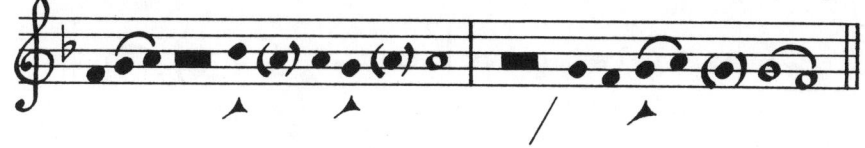

1 *Re - joïce* in the LÓRD, you ríght-eous;*
   it is good for the just / to sing präis-ës.
2 Praise the LÓRD with thé harp;*
   play to him upon the / psal-ter-ÿ and lÿre.

REFRAIN

3 *Sing för* —— hím a néw song;*
   sound a fanfare with all your skill up - / on
                the trüm-pët.
4 For the wórd of the LÓRD is right,*
   and / all his wórks are süre.

REFRAIN

5 *He loves* right-eous-néss and júdg-ment;*
   the loving-kindness of the LORD / fills the
                whöle eärth.
7 He gathers up the waters of the ocean as ín a
                wá-ter-skin*
   and stores up the / depths of the sëa.

REFRAIN

(continued)

BCP, p. 626

REFRAIN

By the word of the Lord were the heav-ens made,

by the breath of his mouth all the heav-en-ly hosts.

PSALM 33   TONE I*f*

8 *Let all* the eárth fear thé LORD;*
    let all who dwell in the world / stand in awe of hïm.

9 For he spóke, and it cáme to pass;*
    he commanded, / and it stóöd fäst.

REFRAIN

10 *The LORD* brings the will of the ná-tions tó naught;*
    he thwarts the designs / of the péö-plës.

11 But the LORD'S will stands fást for év-er,*
    and the designs of his / heart from áğe to äğe.

REFRAIN

Easter Vigil ABC

Refrain

In your light, O God, we see light.

Psalm 36   Tone VI

5 *Your love*, O LORD, reaches to / the héav-ens,*
   and your faith - / ful-nëss tó the clouds.
6 Your righteousness is like the strong mountains,
   your justice like / the gréat deep;*
   you save both / man aňd beást, O LORD.

REFRAIN

7 *How price* - less is / your lóve, O God!*
   your people take refuge under the
                    sha - / dow öf yoúr wings.
8 They feast upon the abun - / dance óf your house;*
   you give them drink from the riv - / er öf yoúr
                    de-lights.

REFRAIN

9 *For with* you is / the wéll of life,*
   and in / your líght wé see light.
10 Continue your loving-kindness to those / who knów you,*
   and your favor to those / who aře trúe of heart.

REFRAIN

EASTER VIGIL ABC

REFRAIN

The Lord of hosts is with us;

the God of Ja-cob is our strong-hold.

PSALM 46   TONE VIII*g*

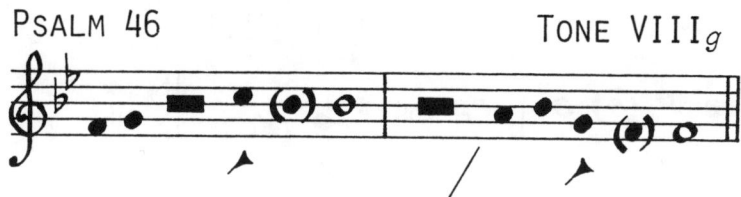

1 *God is* our refuge and stréngth,*
   a very present / help in tróu-ble.
2 Therefore we will not fear, though the eárth be moved,*
   and though the mountains be toppled into
                the / depths of thé sea.
3 Though its waters ráge and foam,*
   and though the mountains tremble / at its tú-mult.

                              REFRAIN

5 *There is* a river whose streams make glad the
                city of Gód,*
   the holy habitation / of the Móst High.
6 God is in the midst of her;
   she shall not be ó-ver-thrown;*
   God shall help her / at the bréak of day.
7 The nations make much ado, and the kingdoms
                are shák-en;*
   God has spoken, and the / earth shall mélt a-way.

                              REFRAIN

(continued)

REFRAIN

The Lord of hosts is with us;

the God   of Ja - cob is our strong-hold.

PSALM 46   **TONE VIII**$_g$

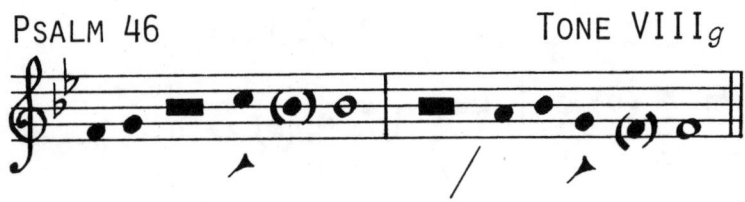

9 *Come now* and look upon the works of the LÓRD,*
    what awesome things / he has dóne on earth.
10 It is he who makes war to cease in áll the world;*
    he breaks the bow, and shatters the spear,
    and / burns the shiélds with fire.
11 "Be still, then, and know that Í am God;*
    I will be exalted among the nations;
    I will be ex - / alt-ed ín the earth."

                      REFRAIN

EASTER VIGIL ABC

REFRAIN

Hap-py is the na-tion whose God is the Lord.

PSALM 33   TONE VI

13 *The LORD* looks down / from héav-en,*
     and beholds all the / peo-plë ín the world.
14 From where he sits enthroned / he túrns his gaze*
     on all / who dẅell ón the earth.
15 He fashions all / the heárts of them*
     and un - / der-ständs áll their works.

REFRAIN

16 *There is* no king that can be saved by a might - / y
                        ár-my;*
     a strong man is not delivered / by his gréat strength.
18 Behold, the eye of the LORD is upon those / who
                        féar him,*
     on those who wait / up-ön hís love,
19 To pluck / their líves from death,*
     and to feed them in / time öf fám-ine.

REFRAIN

20 *Our soul* waits / for thé LORD;*
     he is our / help and oúr shield.
21 Indeed, our heart rejoic - / es ín him,*
     for in his holy / Name wë pút our trust.
22 Let your loving-kindness, O LORD, be / up-ón us,*
     as we have / put oür trúst in you.

REFRAIN

EASTER VIGIL ABC

REFRAIN

Pro-tect me, O God, for I take ref-uge in you.

PSALM 16   TONE VI

5 *O LÖRD*, you are my por - / tion and my cup;*
   it is you / who up-hóld my lot.
6 My boundaries enclose / a pléas-ant land;*
   indeed, I have a / good-lÿ hér-i-tage.

                                    REFRAIN

8 *I have* set the LORD always / be-fóre me;*
   because he is at my right / hand Ï sháll not fall.
9 My heart, therefore, is glad, and my spirit / re-jóic-es;*
   my body al - / so shäll rést in hope.

                                    REFRAIN

10 *For yöu* will not abandon / me tó the grave,*
    nor let your ho - / ly one sée the Pit.
11 You will show me / the páth of life;*
    in your presence there is fullness of joy,
    and in your right hand are pleas - / ures för
                    év-er-more.

                                    REFRAIN

EASTER VIGIL ABC

REFRAIN

I will sing to the Lord,

for he has ris-en up in might.

CANTICLE 8   TONE VIII*g*

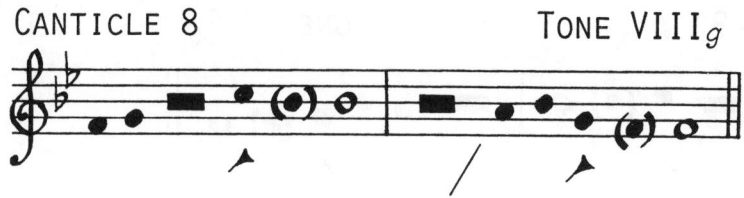

1 *I will* sing to the Lord, for he is lofty and up-líft-ed;*
    the horse and its rider has he / hurled in-tó the sea.
2 The Lord is my strength and my réf-uge;*
    the Lord has be - / come my Sáv-ior.

REFRAIN

3 *This is* my God and I will práise him,*
    the God of my people and I / will ex-ált him.
4 The Lord is a mighty wár-rior;*
    —— / Yah-weh iś his Name.

REFRAIN

5 *The char* - iots of Pharaoh and his army has he
                hurled into the séa;*
    the finest of those who bear armor have been
                drowned / in the Réd Sea.
6 The fathomless deep has over-whélmed them;*
    they sank into the / depths like á stone.

REFRAIN

(continued)

BCP, p. 85

EASTER VIGIL ABC   (continuation)

REFRAIN

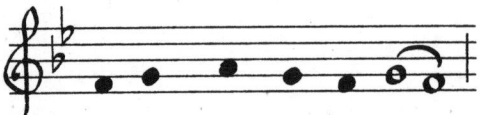

I will sing to the Lord,

for he has ris-en up in might.

CANTICLE 8   TONE VIII*g*

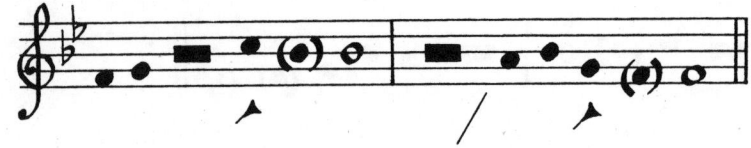

7 *Your right* hand, O Lord, is glorious in míght;*
      your right hand, O Lord, has over - / thrown
                  the én-e-my.
8 Who can be compared with you, O Lord, among the góds?*
      who is like you, glorious in holiness,
      awesome in renown, and work - / er of wón-ders?

                                        REFRAIN

9 *You stretched* forth your ríght hand;*
      the earth / swal-lowed thém up.
10 With your constant love you led the people yóu
                  re-deemed;*
      with your might you brought them in safety to
                  your / ho-ly dwéll-ing.

                                        REFRAIN

11 *You will* bring them in and plánt them*
      on the mount of / your pos-sés-sion,
12 The resting-place you have made for your-sélf, O Lord,*
      the sanctuary, O Lord, that your hand / has
                  es-táb-lished.
13 The Lórd shall reign*
      for ev - / er and év-er.   REFRAIN
                                          BCP, p. 85

EASTER VIGIL ABC

REFRAIN

Pray for the peace of Je-ru-sa-lem.

PSALM 122

TONE VI

1 *I wäs* glad when / they sáid to me,*
   "Let us go to / the hoüse óf the LORD."
2 Now our feet / are stánd-ing*
   within your gates, / O Jë-rú-sa-lem.

REFRAIN

3 *Je-rü-* sa-lem is built as / a cít-y*
   that is at u- / ni-tÿ wíth it-self;
4 To which the tribes go up,
   the tribes of / the LÓRD,*
   the assembly of Israel,
   to praise / the Näme óf the LORD.

REFRAIN

6 *Pray för* the peace of / Je-rú-sa-lem:*
   "May they pros – / per whö lóve you.
7 Peace be / with-ín your walls*
   and quietness with – / in yoür tów-ers.

REFRAIN

8 *For mÿ* brethren and / com-pán-ions' sake,*
   I pray for / your prös-pér-i-ty.
9 Because of the house of / the LÓRD our God,*
   I will / seek tö dó you good."

REFRAIN

BCP, p. 779

Easter Vigil ABC

Refrain

You shall draw wa-ter with re - joic-ing

from the springs of sal-va - tion.

Canticle 9   Tone VIII*g*

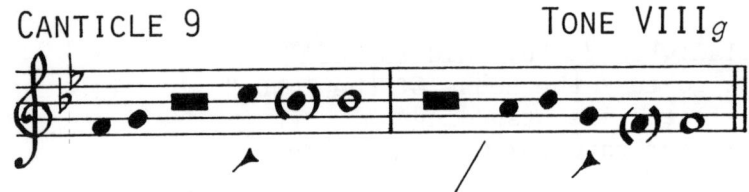

1 *Sure - ly*, it is God who sáves me;*
   I will trust in him and / not be á-fraid.
2 For the Lord is my stronghold and my súre de-fense,*
   and he will / be my Sáv-ior.

REFRAIN

4 *And on* that day you shall sáy,*
   Give thanks to the Lord and / call up-ón his Name;
5 Make his deeds known among the péo-ples;*
   see that they remember that his Name / is ex-ált-ed.

REFRAIN

6 *Sing the* praises of the Lord, for he has done
             gréat things,*
   and this is / known in áll the world.
7 Cry aloud, inhabitants of Zion, ring out your jóy,*
   for the great one in the midst of you is
             the Holy / One of Ís-ra-el.

REFRAIN

BCP, p. 86

Easter Vigil ABC

REFRAIN

As the deer longs for the wa-ter-brooks,

so longs my soul for you, O God.

PSALM 42   **TONE VIII**g

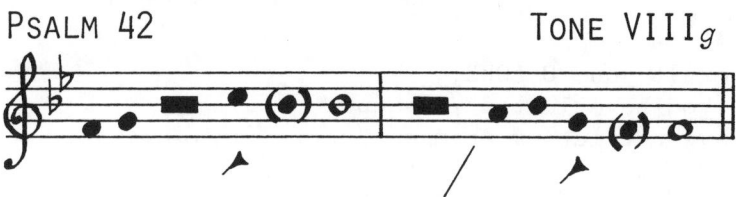

2 *My soul* is athirst for God, athirst for the
                          lív-ing God;*
    when shall I come to appear before the / pres-ence
                          óf God?
3 My tears have been my food dáy and night,*
    while all day long they say to me,
    / "Where is nów your God?"   REFRAIN

4 *I pour* out my soul when I think on these thíngs:*
    how I went with the multitude and led them
                          in - / to the hoúse of God,
5 With the voice of praise and thánks-giv-ing,*
    among those / who keep hó-ly-day.
                                              REFRAIN

6 *Why are* you so full of heaviness, Ó my soul?*
    and why are you so disquiet - / ed with-ín me?
7 Put your trust in Gód;*
    for I will yet give thanks to him,
    who is the help of my coun - / te-nance, ánd my God.
                                              REFRAIN

BCP, p. 643

EASTER VIGIL ABC

REFRAIN

You brought me up, O Lord, from the dead.

PSALM 30   TONE VI

1 *I wïll* exalt you, O LORD,
   because you have lifted / me úp*
      and have not let my enemies / tri-uṁph ó-ver me.
2 O LORD my God, I / cried oút to you,*
      and you / re-störed mé to health.
3 You brought me up, O LORD, from / the deád;*
      you restored my life as I was go - / ing döwn tó
         the grave.

                                                   REFRAIN

4 *Sing tö* the LORD, you servants / of hís;*
      give thanks for the remembrance / of his hó-li-ness.
5 For his wrath endures but the twinkling of / an eýe,*
      his favor / for ä lífe-time.
6 Weeping may spend / the níght,*
      but joy comes / in thë mórn-ing.

                                                   REFRAIN

12 *You häve* turned my wailing in - / to dánc-ing;*
      you have put off my sack-cloth / and clöthed mé
         with joy.
13 Therefore my heart sings to you with - / out ceás-ing;*
      O LORD my God, I will give you / thanks för év-er.

                                                   REFRAIN

EASTER VIGIL ABC

REFRAIN

Re-vive me, O Lord, for your Name's sake.

PSALM 143   TONE VI

1 *LORD, hëar* my prayer,
    and in your faithfulness heed my sup - / pli-cá-tions;*
        answer me / in yöur ríght-eous-ness.
2 Enter not into judgment with / your sér-vant,*
        for in your sight shall no one liv - / ing
                    bë jús-ti-fied.

REFRAIN

4 *My spïr* - it faints / with-ín me;*
        my heart within / me ïs dés-o-late.
5 I remember the time past;
    I muse up - / on áll your deeds;*
        I consider / the wörks óf your hands.

REFRAIN

6 *I sprëad* out / my hánds to you;*
        my soul gasps to you / like ä thírst-y land.
7 O LORD, make haste to answer me; my spir - / it fáils me;*
        do not hide your face from me
        or I shall be like those who / go döwn tó the Pit.

REFRAIN

8 *Let më* hear of your loving-kindness in the morning,
    for I put / my trúst in you;*
        show me the road that I must walk,
        for I lift / up mÿ sóul to you.
10 Teach me to do what pleases you, for you / are mÿ God;*
        let your good Spirit lead / me ön lév-el ground.

REFRAIN
BCP, p. 798

Easter Vigil ABC

REFRAIN

Shout with joy to the Lord, all you lands;

lift up your voice, re-joice, and sing.

PSALM 98   **TONE VIIIc**

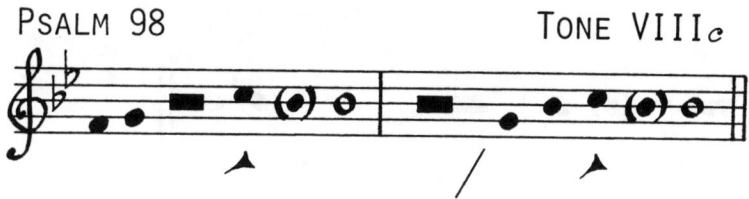

1   *Sing to* the LORD a néw song,*
       for he / has done már-velous things.
2   With his right hand and his hó-ly arm*
       has he won for him - / self the víc-to-ry.

REFRAIN

3   *The LORD* has made known his víc-to-ry;*
       his righteousness has he openly shown in
                       the sight / of the ná-tions.
4   He remembers his mercy and faithfulness to
                       the house of Iś-ra-el,*
       and all the ends of the earth have seen the
                       vic - / to-ry óf our God.

REFRAIN

6   *Sing to* the LORD with the hárp,*
       with the harp / and the vóice of song.
7   With trumpets and the sound of the hórn*
       shout with joy be - / fore the Kíng, the LORD.

REFRAIN

(continued)

BCP, p. 727

REFRAIN

Shout with joy to the Lord, all you lands;

lift up your voice, re-joice, and sing.

PSALM 98   TONE VIIIc

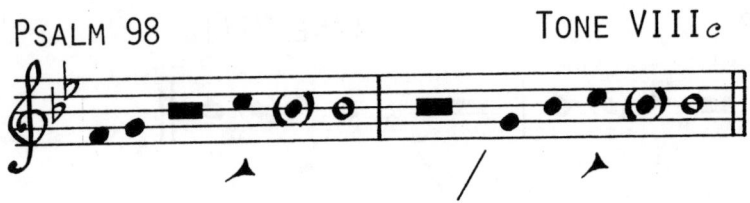

8 *Let the* sea make a noise and all that is ín it,*
    the lands and / those who dwéll there-in.
9 Let the rivers cláp their hands,*
    and let the hills ring out with joy before the LORD,
    when he / comes to júdge the earth.

REFRAIN

Easter Vigil ABC

Refrain

The Lord has done great things for us,

and we are glad in-deed.

Psalm 126   Tone VIII*g*

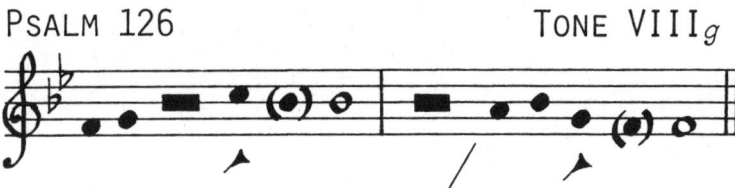

1 *When the* LORD restored the fortunes of Zí-on,*
   then were / we like thóse who dream.
2 Then was our mouth filled with laúgh-ter,*
   and our / tongue with shóuts of joy.

                                                    REFRAIN

3 *Then they* said among the ná-tions,*
   "The LORD has / done great thíngs for them."
4 The LORD has done great thíngs for us,*
   and / we are glád in-deed.

                                                    REFRAIN

5 *Re - store* our fortunes, O LÓRD,*
   like the watercourses / of the Né-gev.
6 Those who sowed with teárs*
   will / reap with sóngs of joy.

                                                    REFRAIN

7 *Those who* go out weeping, carrying the seéd,*
   will come again with joy, shoul - / der-ing
                   théir sheaves.

                                                    REFRAIN

EASTER DAY ABC - *At an Early Service*

One of the Old Testament lessons from the Great Vigil of Easter is used, followed by the corresponding Psalm or Canticle.

EASTER DAY ABC - *At the Vigil or Early Service*

THE GREAT ALLELUIA

After the Epistle, this Alleluia is traditionally sung three times by the Celebrant or by a Cantor, at successively higher pitches, the Congregation repeating it each time.

V.&R. Al - le - - - lu - - ia.

V.&R. Al - le - - - lu - - ia.

V.&R. Al - le - - - lu - - ia.

Followed by:

REFRAIN   **ALLELUIA VII**

Hal-le-lu-jah, hal-le-lu-jah, hal-le-lu-jah!

PSALM 114   **TONE VII*b***

1 *When Is̈* - rael came oút of É-gypt,*
    the house of Jacob from a péo-ple of stránge speech,
2 Judah became God's sánc-tu-ár-y*
    and Israel hís do-mín-ion.

    (continued)

                   REFRAIN

                   BCP, p. 756

REFRAIN   ALLELUIA VII

Hal-le-lu-jah, hal-le-lu-jah, hal - le - lu-jah!

PSALM 114   TONE VII*b*

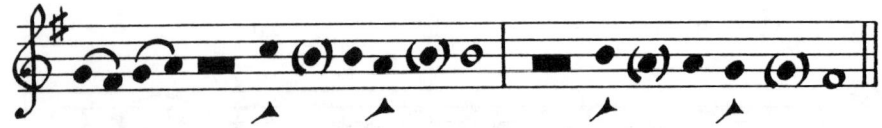

3 *The sea* be-héld it ánd fled;*
   Jordan túrned and wént back.
4 The móun-tains skípped like rams,*
   and the little hílls like yoúng sheep.

                                          REFRAIN

5 *What aïled* you, O séa, that yóu fled?*
   O Jordan, thát you túrned back?
6 You mountains, thát you skípped like rams?*
   you little hílls like yoúng sheep?

                                          REFRAIN

7 *Trem-ble*, O earth, at the prés-ence óf the Lord,*
   at the presence of the Gód of Já-cob,
8 Who turned the hard rock into a poól of wá-ter*
   and flint-stone in-tó a flów-ing spring.

                                          REFRAIN

                    IF PREFERRED, THE PSALM MAY
                  BE SUNG WITHOUT THE REFRAIN
                    (SEE THE FOLLOWING PAGE)

PSALM 114   TONE VII♭

1 *Häl - lë -* lujah!
   When Israel came oút of É-gypt,*
      the house of Jacob from a péo-ple of stránge speech,

2 Judah became God's sánc-tu-ár-y*
      and Israel hís do-mín-ion.

3 The sea be-héld it ánd fled;*
      Jordan túrned and wént back.

4 The móun-tains skípped like rams,*
      and the little hílls like yoúng sheep.

5 What ailed you, O séa, that yóu fled?*
      O Jordan, thát you túrned back?

6 You mountains, thát you skípped like rams?*
      you little hílls like yoúng sheep?

7 Tremble, O earth, at the prés-ence óf the Lord,*
      at the presence of the Gód of Já-cob,

8 Who turned the hard rock into a poól of wá-ter*
      and flint-stone in-tó a flów-ing spring.

REFRAIN

On this day the Lord has act-ed;

we will re-joice and be glad in it.

PSALM 118   TONE VIII*g*

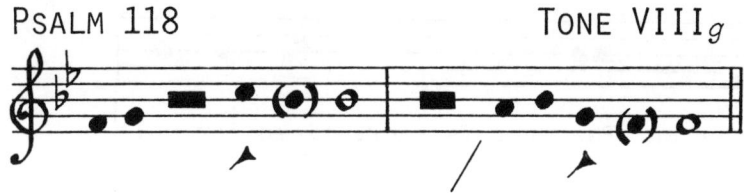

14 *The LORD* is my strength and my sóng,*
      and he has become / my sal-vá-tion.
15 There is a sound of exultation and víc-to-ry*
      in the tents / of the ríght-eous.

                                    REFRAIN

16 "*The right* hand of the LORD has trí-umphed!*
      the right hand of the LORD is exaltéd!
      the right hand of the / LORD has trí-umphed!"
17 I shall not die, but líve,*
      and declare the / works of thé LORD.

                                    REFRAIN

22 *The same* stone which the builders re-jéct-ed*
      has become / the chief cór-ner-stone.
23 This is the LORD'S dó-ing,*
      and it is mar - / vel-ous ín our eyes.

                                    REFRAIN

EASTER DAY C - *Principal Service (morning)*

ALLELUIA VIII

Al-le - lu - ia, al-le-lu - ia, al - le-lu-ia.

VERSE (1 Cor. 5:7,8)   TONE VIII*g*

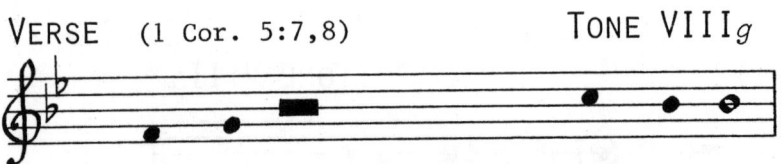

Christ our Passover is sacri-ficed for us:*

therefore let us keep the feast.

REFRAIN   ALLELUIA VII

Hal-le-lu - jah, hal - le - lu - jah, hal - le - lu-jah!

PSALM 114   TONE VIIb

1 *Häl - lë* - lujah!
   When Israel came oút of É-gypt,*
      the house of Jacob from a péo-ple of stránge speech,
2 Judah became God's sánc-tu-ár-y*
      and Israel hís do-mín-ion.

                                                     REFRAIN

3 *The sëa* be-héld it ánd fled;*
      Jordan túrned and wént back.
4 The móun-tains skípped like rams,*
      and the little hílls like yoúng sheep.

                                                     REFRAIN

5 *Whät aïled* you, O séa, that yóu fled?*
      O Jordan, thát you túrned back?
6 You mountains, thát you skípped like rams?*
      you little hílls like yoúng sheep?

                                                     REFRAIN

7 *Trëm - blë*, O earth, at the prés-ence óf the Lord,*
      at the presence of the Gód of Já-cob,
8 Who turned the hard rock into a poól of wá-ter*
      and flint-stone in-tó a flów-ing spring.

                                                     REFRAIN

        ALLELUIA AS AT PRINCIPAL SERVICE
                  (MORNING)

EASTER DAY ABC - *Evening Service*

REFRAIN

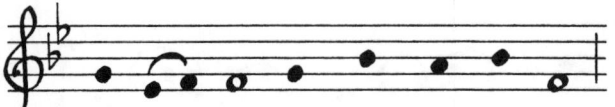

On this day the Lord has act-ed;

we will re-joice and be glad in it.

PSALM 118   TONE VIIIg

14 *The LORD* is my strength and my sóng,*
        and he has become / my sal-vá-tion.
15 There is a sound of exultation and víc-to-ry*
        in the tents / of the ríght-eous.

                                    REFRAIN

16 "*The right* hand of the LORD has trí-umphed!*
        the right hand of the LORD is exalted!
        the right hand of the / LORD has trí-umphed!"
17 I shall not die, but líve,*
        and declare the / works of thé LORD.

                                    REFRAIN

22 *The same* stone which the builders re-jéct-ed*
        has become / the chief cór-ner-stone.
23 This is the LORD'S dó-ing,*
        and it is mar - / vel-ous ín our eyes.

                                    REFRAIN

        ALLELUIA AS AT PRINCIPAL SERVICE
                (MORNING)

EASTER DAY ABC - *Evening Service*

REFRAIN

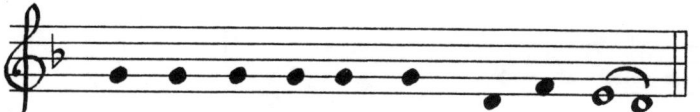

For his mer-cy en-dures for ev - er.

PSALM 136   *Tonus Peregrinus*

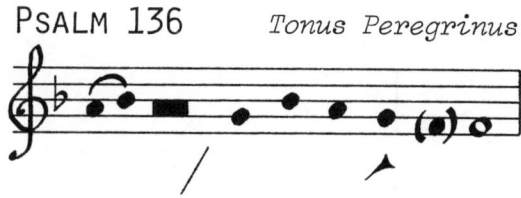

1 *Give* thanks to / the LORD, for hé is good,*

> REFRAIN

2 *Give* thanks / to the God óf gods,*

> REFRAIN

3 *Give* thanks / to the Lord óf lords,*

> REFRAIN

10 *Who* struck down the / first-born of É-gypt,*

> REFRAIN

11 *And* brought out Isra - / el from a-móng them,*

> REFRAIN

12 *With* a mighty / hand and a strétched-out arm,*

> REFRAIN

13 *Who* divided / the Red Sea ín two,*

> REFRAIN

14 *And* made Israel to / pass through the mídst of it,*

> REFRAIN

15 *But* swept Pharaoh and his army / in-to the Réd Sea,*

> REFRAIN

(continued)

REFRAIN

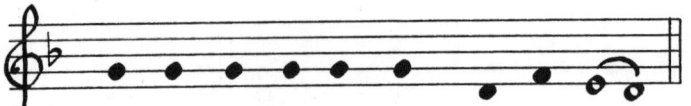

For his mer-cy en-dures for ev - er.

PSALM 136   *Tonus Peregrinus*

16 *Who* led his peo - / ple through the wíl-der-ness,*

                                    REFRAIN

23 *Who* remembered / us in our lów es-tate,*

                                      REFRAIN

24 *And* delivered / us from our én-e-mies,*

                                      REFRAIN

25 *Who* gives / food to all créa-tures,*

                                      REFRAIN

26 *Give* thanks to / the God of héav-en,*

                                      REFRAIN

REFRAIN   ALLELUIA VIII

Hal-le - lu - jah, hal-le-lu - jah, hal - le-lu-jah!

PSALM 16   TONE VIII*g*

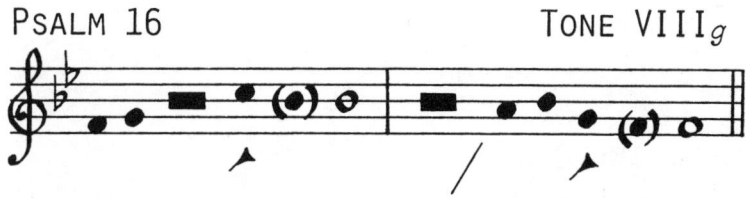

8   *I have* set the LORD always be-fóre me;*
    because he is at my right / hand I shàll not fall.

                                          REFRAIN

9   *My heart*, therefore, is glad, and my spirit
                    re-joíc-es;*
    my body al - / so shall rést in hope.

                                          REFRAIN

10 *For you* will not abandon me to the gráve,*
    nor let your ho - / ly one sée the Pit.

                                          REFRAIN

11 *You will* show me the páth of life;*
    in your presence there is fullness of joy,
    and in your right hand are pleas - / ures for
                    év-er-more.

                                          REFRAIN

              IN PLACE OF THE PSALM,
        AN ALLELUIA VERSE MAY BE USED.
              (SEE NEXT PAGE)

BCP, p. 600

ALLELUIA VIII

Al-le - lu - ia, al-le-lu - ia, al - le-lu-ia.

VERSE   (Psalm 118:24)

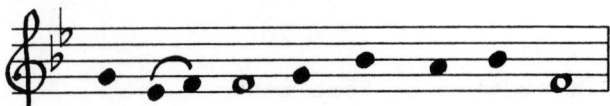

On this day the Lord has act-ed;*

we will re-joice and be glad in it.

Monday in Easter Week ABC

Refrain

Give thanks to the Lord, for he is good;

his mer-cy en-dures for ev-er.

Alternate Refrain　　　Alleluia VIII

Hal-le - lu - jah, hal-le-lu - jah, hal - le-lu-jah!

Psalm 118　　　Tone VIIIg

19　*O - pen* for me the gates of ríght-eous-ness;*
　　I will enter them;
　　I will offer / thanks tǫ thé LORD.
20　"This is the gate of the LÓRD;*
　　he who is right - / eous may én-ter."

　　　　　　　　　　　　　　　　　REFRAIN

21　*I will* give thanks to you, for you án-swered me*
　　and have become / my sal-vá-tion.
22　The same stone which the builders re-jéct-ed*
　　has become / the chief cór-ner-stone.

　　　　　　　　　　　　　　　　　REFRAIN

(continued)

REFRAIN

Give thanks to the Lord, for he is good;

his mer-cy en-dures for ev-er.

ALTERNATE REFRAIN   ALLELUIA VIII

Hal-le - lu - jah, hal-le-lu - jah, hal - le-lu-jah!

PSALM 118   TONE VIII*g*

23 *This is* the LORD'S dó-ing,*
    and it is mar - / vel-ous ín our eyes.
24 On this day the LORD has áct-ed;*
    we will rejoice / and be glád in it.

REFRAIN

IN PLACE OF THE PSALM,
AN ALLELUIA VERSE MAY BE USED.
(SEE NEXT PAGE)

Alleluia VIII

Al-le - lu - ia, al-le-lu - ia, al - le-lu-ia.

Verse   (Psalm 118:24)

On this day the Lord has act-ed;*

we will re-joice and be glad in it.

REFRAIN   ALLELUIA VI

Hal-le-lu-jah, hal-le-lu-jah, hal-le-lu-jah!

PSALM 33   TONE VI

1 *Re - joice* in the LORD, / you ríght-eous;*
   it is good for the just / to sïng práis-es.
2 Praise the LORD / with thé harp;*
   play to him upon the psal - / te-rÿ añd lyre.

                                              REFRAIN

18 *Be - hold*, the eye of the LORD is upon those / who
                      féar him,*
    on those who / wait üp-ón his love,
19 To pluck / their líves from death,*
    and to feed them in / time öf fám-ine.

                                              REFRAIN

20 *Our soul* waits / for thé LORD;*
    he is our / help añd oúr shield.
21 Indeed, our heart rejoic - / es ín him,*
    for in his holy / Name wë pút our trust.

                                              REFRAIN

                  IN PLACE OF THE PSALM,
            AN ALLELUIA VERSE MAY BE USED,
            OR PSALM 118 AS ON MONDAY.

                  ALLELUIA AS ON MONDAY

                                              BCP, p. 626

REFRAIN　　　　　　　　　　　　**ALLELUIA VII**

Hal-le-lu - jah, hal - le - lu - jah, hal - le - lu-jah!

PSALM 105　　　　　　　　　　　　**TONE VIIb**

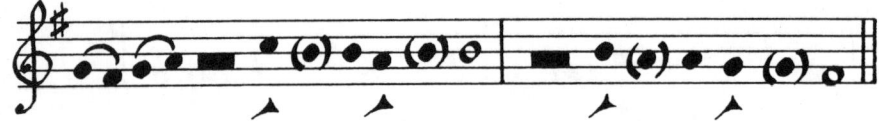

1 *Give thánks* to the LORD and cáll up-ón his Name;*
    make known his deeds a-móng the péo-ples.
2 Sing to him, sing práis-es tó him,*
    and speak of áll his már-velous works.

                                        REFRAIN

3 *Glo - rŷ* —— ín his hó-ly Name;*
    let the hearts of those who seék the LÓRD re-joice.
4 Search for the LÓRD and hís strength;*
    con-tín-ual-ly seék his face.

                                        REFRAIN

5 *Re - mem* - ber the már-vels hé has done,*
    his wonders and the júdg-ments óf his mouth,
6 O offspring of A-bra-hám his sér-vant,*
    O children of Já-cob his chó-sen.

                                        REFRAIN

7 —— He ís the LÓRD our God;*
    his judgments pre-váil in áll the world.
8 He has always been mindful óf his cóv-e-nant,*
    the promise he made for a thousand gén-er-á-tions.

                                        REFRAIN

IN PLACE OF THE PSALM,
AN ALLELUIA VERSE MAY BE USED,
OR PSALM 118 AS ON MONDAY.

ALLELUIA AS ON MONDAY

BCP, p. 738

REFRAIN   ALLELUIA VII

Hal-le-lu - jah, hal - le - lu - jah, hal - le - lu-jah!

PSALM 8   TONE VIIb

1 —— O LÓRD our Góv-er-nor,*
     how exalted is your Náme in áll the world!
2 Out of the mouths of ín-fants and chíl-dren*
     your majesty is praised a-bóve the héav-ens.

                                        REFRAIN

4 *When Ï* consider your heavens, the wórk of your fín-gers,*
     the moon and the stars you have sét in their cóur-ses,
5 What is man that you should be mínd-ful óf him?*
     the son of man that yóu should seék him out?

                                        REFRAIN

6 *You häve* made him but little lower thán the án-gels;*
     you adorn him with gló-ry and hón-or;
7 You give him mastery over the wórks of yóur hands;*
     you put all things ún-der hís feet.

                                        REFRAIN

            IN PLACE OF THE PSALM,
      AN ALLELUIA VERSE MAY BE USED,
      OR PSALM 118 AS ON MONDAY.

          ALLELUIA AS ON MONDAY

REFRAIN   ALLELUIA VII

Hal-le-lu-jah, hal-le-lu-jah, hal-le-lu-jah!

PSALM 114   TONE VII♭

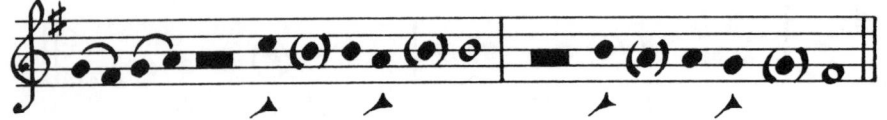

1 *When Is* - rael came oút of É-gypt,*
      the house of Jacob from a péo-ple of stránge speech,
2 Judah became God's sánc-tu-ár-y*
      and Israel hís do-mín-ion.   REFRAIN

3 *The sea* be-héld it añd fled;*
      Jordan túrned and wént back.
4 The moún-tains skípped like rams,*
      and the little hílls like yoúng sheep.

                                                    REFRAIN

5 *What aïled* you, O séa, that yóu fled?*
      O Jordan, thát you túrned back?
6 You mountains, thát you skípped like rams?*
      you little hílls like yoúng sheep?

                                                    REFRAIN

7 *Trem - bḷe*, O earth, at the prés-ence óf the Lord,*
      at the presence of the Gód of Já-cob,
8 Who turned the hard rock into a poól of wá-ter*
      and flint-stone in-tó a flów-ing spring.

                                                    REFRAIN

            IN PLACE OF THE PSALM,
        AN ALLELUIA VERSE MAY BE USED,
        OR PSALM 118 AS ON MONDAY.

        ALLELUIA AS ON MONDAY

                                        BCP, p. 756

FRIDAY IN EASTER WEEK ABC

REFRAIN   ALLELUIA VIII

Hal-le-lu-jah, hal-le-lu-jah, hal-le-lu-jah!

PSALM 116   TONE VIIIg

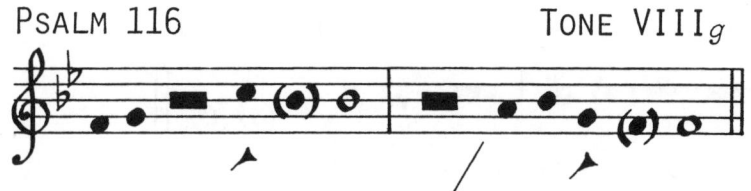

1 *I love* the LORD, because he has heard the voice of
                   my sup-pli-cá-tion,*
   because he has inclined his ear to me whenever
                   I / called up-ón him.

                                        REFRAIN

2 *The cords* of death entangled me;
   the grip of the grave took hóld of me;*
   I came to / grief and sór-row.
3 Then I called upon the Name of the LÓRD:*
   "O LORD, I / pray you, sáve my life."

                                        REFRAIN

5 *The LORD* watches over the ín-no-cent;*
   I was brought very low, / and he hélped me.
6 Turn again to your rest, Ó my soul,*
   for the LORD has / treat-ed yóu well.

                                        REFRAIN

7 *For you* have rescued my lífe from death,*
   my eyes from tears, and my / feet from stúm-bling.
8 I will walk in the presence of the LÓRD*
   in the land / of the lív-ing.

                                        REFRAIN

            IN PLACE OF THE PSALM,
    AN ALLELUIA VERSE MAY BE USED,
       OR PSALM 118 AS ON MONDAY.

        ALLELUIA AS ON MONDAY
                                        BCP, p. 759

REFRAIN   ALLELUIA VIII

Hal-le - lu - jah, hal-le-lu - jah, hal - le-lu-jah!

PSALM 118   TONE VIII*g*

1 *Give thanks* to the LORD, for hé is good;*
    his mercy en - / dures for év-er.
14 The LORD is my strength and my sóng,*
    and he has become / my sal-vá-tion.

                         REFRAIN

15 *There is* a sound of exultation and víc-to-ry*
    in the tents / of the ríght-eous:
16 "The right hand of the LORD has trí-umphed!*
    the right hand of the LORD is exalted!
    the right hand of the / LORD has trí-umphed!"

                         REFRAIN

17 *I shall* not die, but líve,*
    and declare the / works of thé LORD.
18 The LORD has punished me sóre-ly,*
    but he did not hand me / o-ver tó death.

                         REFRAIN

IN PLACE OF THE PSALM,
AN ALLELUIA VERSE MAY BE USED,
OR PSALM 118 AS ON MONDAY.

ALLELUIA AS ON MONDAY

2 Easter C

REFRAIN

Give thanks to the Lord, for he is good;

his mer-cy en-dures for ev-er.

ALTERNATE REFRAIN   **ALLELUIA VIII**

Hal-le-lu-jah, hal-le-lu-jah, hal-le-lu-jah!

PSALM 118   **TONE VIII**_g_

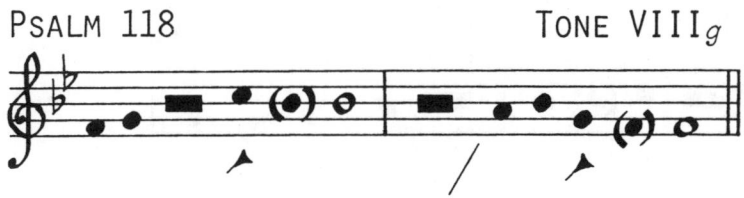

19 *O-pen* for me the gates of ríght-eous-ness;*
    I will enter them;
    I will offer / thanks to thé LORD.
20 "This is the gate of the LÓRD;*
    he who is right - / eous may én-ter."

REFRAIN

21 *I will* give thanks to you, for you án-swered me*
    and have become / my sal-vá-tion.
22 The same stone which the builders re-jéct-ed*
    has become / the chief cór-ner-stone.

REFRAIN

(continued)

REFRAIN

Give thanks to the Lord, for he is good;

his mer-cy en-dures for ev-er.

ALTERNATE REFRAIN   ALLELUIA VIII

Hal-le - lu - jah, hal-le-lu - jah, hal - le-lu-jah!

PSALM 118   TONE VIII*g*

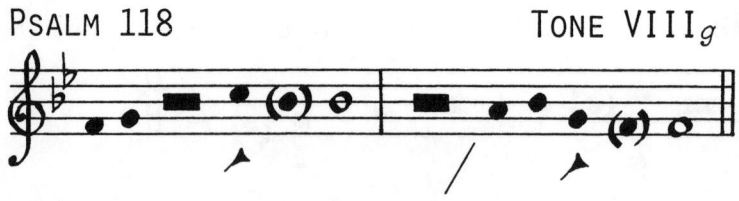

23 *This is* the LORD'S dó-ing,*
       and it is mar - / vel-ous ín our eyes.
24 On this day the LORD has áct-ed;*
       we will rejoice / and be glád in it.

                                    REFRAIN

ALLELUIA VIII

Al-le - lu - ia, al-le-lu - ia, al - le-lu-ia.

VERSE   (John 20:29)   TONE VIII*g*

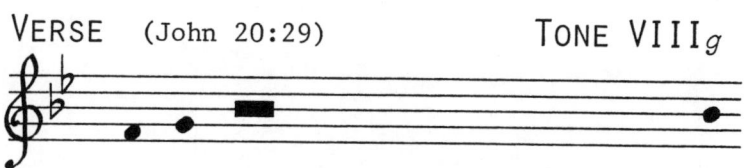

You be - lieve in me, Thomas, because you

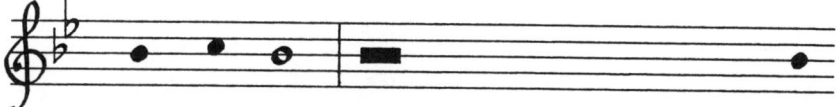

have seen me;* blessed are those who have not

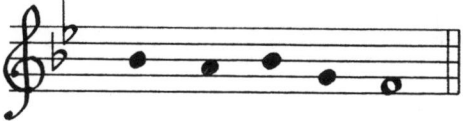

seen and yet be-lieve.

REFRAIN   ALLELUIA IV

Hal-le-lu-jah, hal-le - lu - jah, hal-le - lu-jah!

PSALM 111   TONE IVₑ

1 *Hal - lë - lujah!*
   I will give thanks to the LORD / with my whóle heart,*
      in the assembly of the upright, in / the
                        con-gre̐-g̐a̐-tion.
2 Great are the deeds / of the LÓRD!*
      they are studied by / all who dë-líght ïn them.

                                        REFRAIN

3 *His work* is full of majes - / ty and splén-dor,*
      and his righteous - / ness en-du̐res fór ëv-er.
4 He makes his marvelous works to / be re-mém-bered;*
      the LORD is gracious and / full of c̐öm-pás-sion.

                                        REFRAIN

9 *He sënt* redemption to his people;
      he commanded his cove - / nant for év-er;*
      holy and / awe-some ïs h̐is Name.
10 The fear of the LORD is the begin - / ning of wís-dom;*
      those who act accordingly have a good understanding;
      his praise / en-dures för ëv-er.

                                        REFRAIN

ALLELUIA VII

Al-le-lu - ia, al - le - lu - ia, al - le - lu-ia.

VERSE   (John 20:29)   TONE VIIb

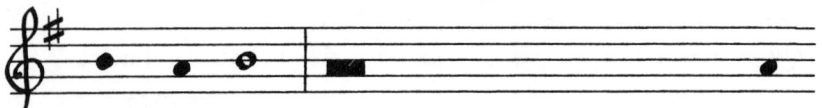

You be - lieve in me, Thomas, be-cause you

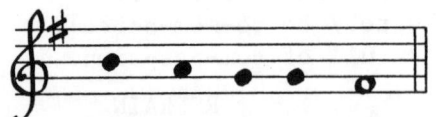

have seen me;* blessed are those who have not

seen and yet be-lieve.

3 EASTER C

REFRAIN

Sing to the Lord a new song.

ALTERNATE REFRAIN　　　　**ALLELUIA III**

Hal-le - lu - jah, hal-le - lu-jah, hal-le - lu-jah!

PSALM 33　　　　**TONE IIIᵇ**

1 *Re - joice* in the LÓRD, you ríght-eous;*
   it is good for the just to / sing práis-es.
3 Sing for hím a néw song;*
   sound a fanfare with all your skill upon / the
      trúm-pet.

　　　　　　　　　　　　　　REFRAIN

4 *For the* —— wórd of the LÓRD ïs right,*
   and all / his wórks are sure.
5 He loves righteous-néss and jús-tice;*
   the loving-kindness of the LORD fills / the
      whóle earth.

　　　　　　　　　　　　　　REFRAIN

10 *The LORD* brings the will of the ná-tions tö naught;*
   he thwarts the designs of / the péo-ples.
11 But the LORD'S will stands fást for év-er,*
   and the designs of his heart / from aǧe to age.

　　　　　　　　　　　　　　REFRAIN

3 EASTER C

ALLELUIA I

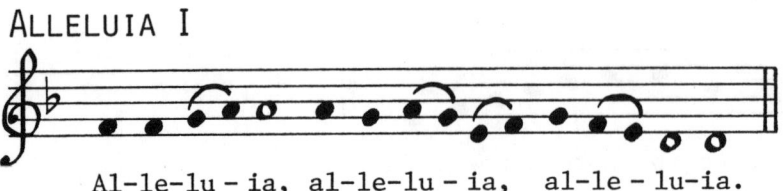

Al-le-lu - ia, al-le-lu - ia, al-le - lu-ia.

VERSE (Rom. 6:9)   TONE I*f*

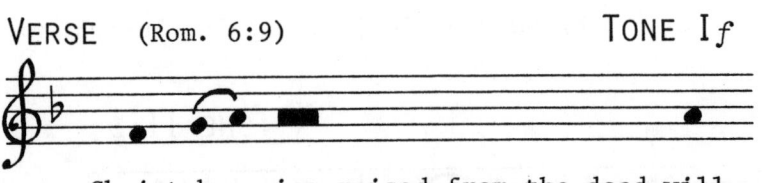

Christ be - ing raised from the dead will

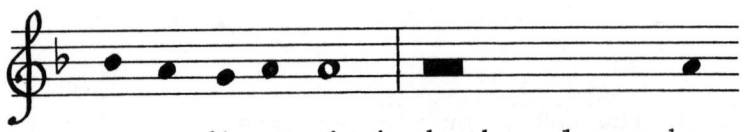

nev-er die a-gain;* death no longer has

do-min-ion o - ver him.

4 EASTER C

REFRAIN

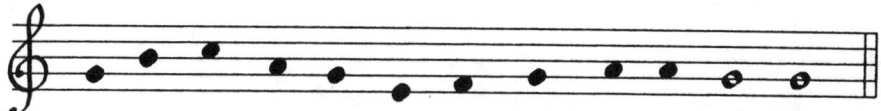

We are his peo-ple and the sheep of his pas-ture.

ALTERNATE REFRAIN   ALLELUIA VIII

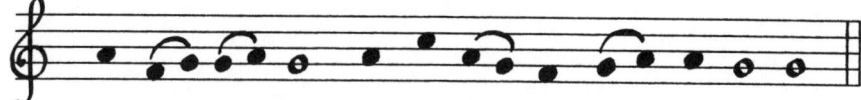

Hal-le - lu - jah, hal-le-lu - jah, hal - le-lu-jah!

PSALM 100   TONE VIII*g*

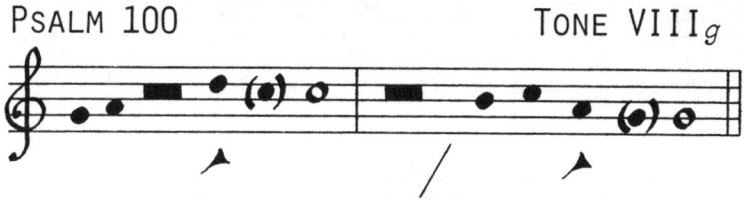

1 *Be joy* - ful in the LORD, áll you lands;*
   serve the LORD with gladness
   and come before his / pres-ence wíth a song.

                                        REFRAIN

2 *Know this:* The LORD him-sélf is God;*
   he himself has made us, and we are his;
   we are his people and the sheep / of his pás-ture.

                                        REFRAIN

3 *En - ter* his gates with thanksgiving;
   go into his coúrts with praise;*
   give thanks to him and / call up-ón his Name.

                                        REFRAIN

4 *For the* LORD is good;
   his mercy is ever-lást-ing;*
   and his faithfulness en - / dures from aǵe to age.

                                        REFRAIN

BCP, p. 729

4 EASTER C

ALLELUIA IV

Al-le-lu-ia, al-le - lu - ia, al-le - lu-ia.

VERSE   (John 10:14)   TONE IV*e*

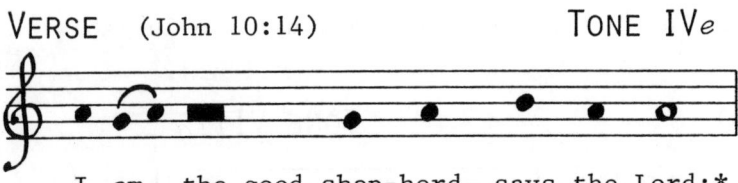

I am   the good shep-herd, says the Lord;*

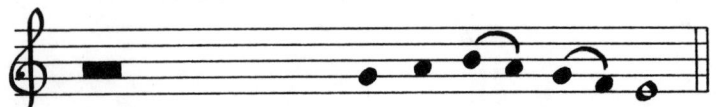

I know my sheep, and my sheep know me.

5 EASTER C

REFRAIN

I will ex - alt you, O God my King,

and bless your Name for ev - er and ev-er.

ALTERNATE REFRAIN   ALLELUIA V

Hal-le-lu-jah, hal-le-lu - jah, hal - le - lu-jah!

PSALM 145   TONE Vₐ

3 *Great is* the LORD and greatly to be praísed;*
   there is no end to his gréat-ness.
4 One generation shall praise your works to an-óth-er*
   and sháll de-cláre your power.

                                        REFRAIN

5 *I will* ponder the glorious splendor of your má-jes-ty*
   and áll your már-velous works.
6 They shall speak of the might of your wón-drous acts,*
   and I will téll of your gréat-ness.

                                        REFRAIN

(continued)

BCP, p. 801

REFRAIN

I will ex-alt you, O God my King,

and bless your Name for ev-er and ev-er.

ALTERNATE REFRAIN   ALLELUIA V

Hal-le-lu-jah, hal-le-lu-jah, hal-le-lu-jah!

PSALM 145   TONE Va

8 *The LORD* is gracious and full of com-pás-sion,*
   slow to anger and óf great kínd-ness.
9 The LORD is loving to eve-ry one*
   and his compassion is ó-ver áll his works.

REFRAIN

Alleluia VII

Al-le-lu - ia, al - le - lu - ia, al - le - lu-ia.

Verse (John 13:34)   Tone VII♭

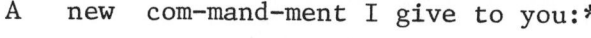

A   new   com-mand-ment I give to you:*

love one another as I have loved you.

REFRAIN

Let the peo-ples praise you, O God, al-le-lu-ia;

let all the peo-ples praise you, al-le-lu-ia.

ALTERNATE REFRAIN   ALLELUIA VI

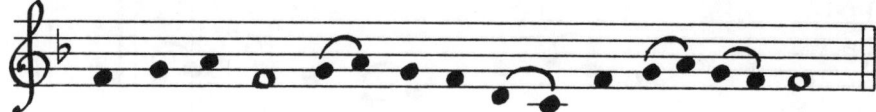

Hal-le-lu-jah, hal - le-lu-jah, hal-le - lu - jah!

PSALM 67   TONE VI

1 *May Gŏd* be merciful to us / and bléss us,*
   show us the light of his counte - / nance and
                      cóme to us.
2 Let your ways be known up - / on eárth,*
   your saving health a - / mong äll ná-tions.

                                        REFRAIN

4 *Let thĕ* nations be glad / and síng for joy,*
   for you judge the peoples with equity
   and guide all the / na-tiöns úp-on earth.

                                        REFRAIN

(continued)

BCP, p. 675

REFRAIN

Let the peo-ples praise you, O God, al-le-lu-ia;

let all the peo-ples praise you, al-le-lu-ia.

ALTERNATE REFRAIN   ALLELUIA VI

Hal-le-lu-jah, hal - le-lu-jah,   hal-le - lu - jah!

PSALM 67   TONE VI

6 *The earth* has brought forth / her ín-crease;*
    may God, our own God, give / us his bléss-ing.
7 May God give us / his bléss-ing,*
    and may all the ends of the earth / stand ïn
            awe of him.

REFRAIN

6 EASTER C

ALLELUIA I

Al-le-lu - ia, al-le-lu - ia, al-le - lu-ia.

VERSE   (John 14:23)   TONE I*f*

If an - y-one loves me, he will keep my word;*

and my Father will love him, and we will

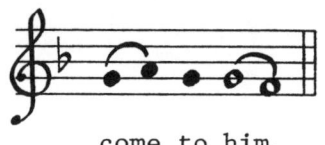

come to him.

Ascension Day C

Refrain

I am with you al-ways, to the close of the age.

Alternate Refrain   Alleluia VIII

Hal-le - lu - jah, hal-le-lu - jah, hal - le-lu-jah!

Psalm 110   Tone VIIIc

1 *The LORD* said to my Lord, "Sit at my ríght hand,*
   until I make your ene - / mies your fóot-stool."

                                       REFRAIN

2 *The LORD* will send the scepter of your power
                   out of Zí-on,*
   saying, "Rule over your enemies / round a-bóut you.

                                         REFRAIN

3 *Prince - ly* state has been yours from the day of
                   your bírth;*
   in the beauty of holiness have I begotten you,
   like dew from the womb / of the mórn-ing."

                                         REFRAIN

4 *The LORD* has sworn and he will nót re-cant:*
   "You are a priest for ever after the order / of
                Mel-chí-ze-dek."

                                       REFRAIN

Ascension Day C

Alleluia IV

Al-le-lu-ia, al-le - lu - ia, al-le - lu-ia.

Verse (Matt. 28:19-20) Tone IV*e*

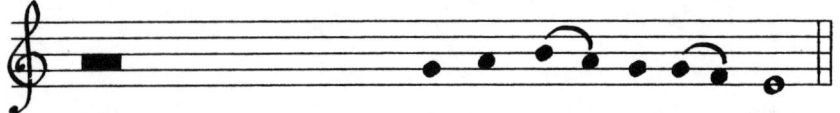

Go and make disciples of all na-tions;*

I am with you always, to the close of the age.

REFRAIN

God has gone up with a   shout, the Lord with

the sound of the ram's-horn.

ALTERNATE REFRAIN   ALLELUIA VII

Hal-le-lu-jah, hal-le-lu-jah, hal-le - lu-jah!

PSALM 47   TONE VII*b*

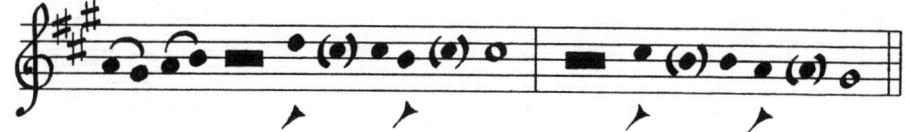

1 *Clap your* hands, all you péo-ples;*
     shout to God with a cry of joy.
2 For the LORD Most High is to be feared;*
     he is the great King o-ver all the earth.

                                  REFRAIN

5 *God has* gone úp with á shout,*
     the LORD with the sound of the rám's-horn.
6 Sing praises to Gód, sing práis-es;*
     sing praises to our Kíng, sing práis-es.

                                  REFRAIN

(continued)

REFRAIN

God has gone up with a shout, the Lord with

the sound of the ram's-horn.

ALTERNATE REFRAIN   ALLELUIA VII

Hal-le-lu-jah, hal-le-lu-jah, hal-le-lu-jah!

PSALM 47   TONE VIIb

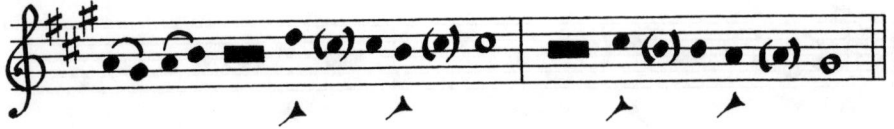

7 *For God* is Kíng of áll the earth;*
     sing práis-es with áll your skill.
8 God reigns ó-ver the ná-tions;*
     God sits up-ón his hó-ly throne.

REFRAIN

Ascension Day C

Alleluia IV

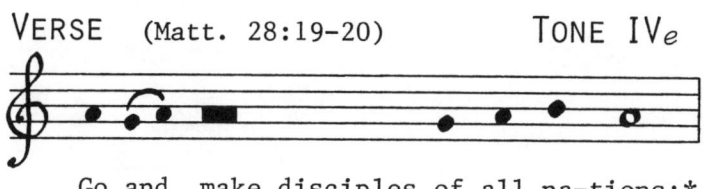

Al-le-lu-ia, al-le - lu - ia, al-le - lu-ia.

Verse (Matt. 28:19-20)   Tone IV*e*

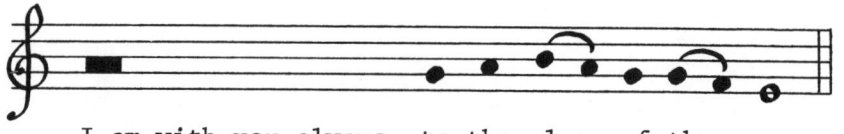

Go and make disciples of all na-tions;*

I am with you always, to the close of the age.

7 EASTER C

REFRAIN

God has gone up with a   shout, the Lord with

the sound of the ram's-horn.

ALTERNATE REFRAIN   ALLELUIA VII

Hal-le-lu-jah, hal-le-lu-jah, hal-le - lu-jah!

PSALM 47   TONE VIIb

1 *Clap your* hands, áll you péo-ples;*
       shout to God wíth a crý of joy.
2 For the LORD Most Hígh is tó be feared;*
       he is the great Kíng o-ver áll the earth.

REFRAIN

5 *Göd häs* gone úp with á shout,*
       the LORD with the soúnd of the rám's-horn.
6 Sing praises to Gód, sing práis-es;*
       sing praises to our Kíng, sing práis-es.

REFRAIN

(continued)

REFRAIN

God has gone up with a   shout, the Lord with

the sound of the ram's-horn.

ALTERNATE REFRAIN   ALLELUIA VII

Hal-le-lu - jah, hal - le - lu - jah, hal - le   - lu-jah!

PSALM 47   TONE VIIb

7 *For God* is Kíng of áll the earth;*
    sing práis-es with áll your skill.
8 God reigns ó-ver the ná-tions;*
    God sits up-ón his hó-ly throne.

REFRAIN

7 Easter C

Alleluia I

Al-le-lu - ia, al-le-lu - ia, al-le - lu-ia.

Verse (John 14:18)   Tone I*f*

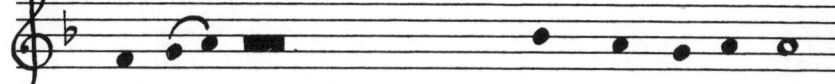

The Lord said, I will not leave you des-o-late;*

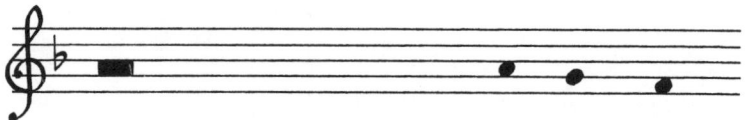

I will come back to you, and your hearts

will re-joice.

7 Easter C

Refrain

Sing to God, O king-doms of the earth;

sing prais-es to the Lord.

Alternate Refrain   Alleluia VII

Hal-le-lu-jah, hal-le-lu-jah, hal-le - lu-jah!

Psalm 68   Tone VIIb

4 *Sing to* God, sing praises to his Name;
   exalt him who rides up-ón the heáv-ens;*
      YAHWEH is his Name, re-jóice be-fóre him!
5 Father of orphans, de-fénd-er of wíd-ows,*
      God in his holy háb-i-tá-tion!

                                        REFRAIN

7 *Ö Göd*, when you went forth be-fóre your péo-ple,*
      when you márched through the wíl-der-ness,
8 The earth shook, and the skies poured down rain,
   at the presence of God, the Gód of Sí-nai,*
      at the presence of God, the Gód of Iś-ra-el.

                                        REFRAIN

(continued)

REFRAIN

Sing to God,   O   king-doms of the earth;

sing prais - es   to   the Lord.

ALTERNATE REFRAIN   ALLELUIA VII

Hal-le-lu - jah, hal - le - lu - jah, hal - le - lu-jah!

PSALM 68   TONE VII*b*

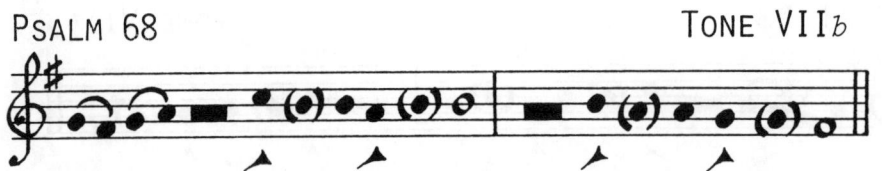

17 *The char* - iots of God are twenty thousand,
    even thóu-sands of thóu-sands;*
        the Lord comes in holi-néss from Sí-nai.
18 You have gone up on high and led captivity captive;
    you have received gifts even fróm your én-e-mies,*
        that the LORD God might dwéll a-móng them.

                                        REFRAIN

Alleluia I

Al-le-lu - ia, al-le-lu - ia, al-le - lu-ia.

Verse   (John 14:18)   Tone I ƒ

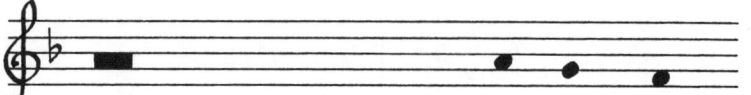

The Lord said, I will not leave you des-o-late;*

I will come back to you, and your hearts

will re-joice.

Vigil of Pentecost ABC   *(or Early Service)*

REFRAIN

Hap-py is the na-tion whose God is the Lord.

PSALM 33   TONE VI

13 *The LORD* looks down / from héav-ën,*
    and beholds all the / peo-plë ín the world.
14 From where he sits enthroned / he túrns his gaze*
    on all / who dwëll ön the earth.
15 He fashions all / the heárts of them*
    and un - / der-ständs áll their works.

REFRAIN

16 *There ïs* no king that can be saved by a might - / y
                ár-my;*
    a strong man is not delivered / by his gréat strength.
18 Behold, the eye of the LORD is upon those / who
                feár him,*
    on those who wait / up-ön hís love,
19 To pluck / their líves from death,*
    and to feed them in / time öf fám-ine.

REFRAIN

20 *Our soül* waits / for thé LORD;*
    he is our / help änd oúr shield.
21 Indeed, our heart rejoic - / es ín him,*
    for in his holy / Name wë pút our trust.
22 Let your loving-kindness, O LORD, be / up-ón us,*
    as we have / put oür trúst in you.

REFRAIN

BCP, p. 627

VIGIL OF PENTECOST ABC   *(or Early Service)*

REFRAIN

He has made us a king-dom of priests

and a ho-ly na-tion.

CANTICLE 13   TONE VIII*g*

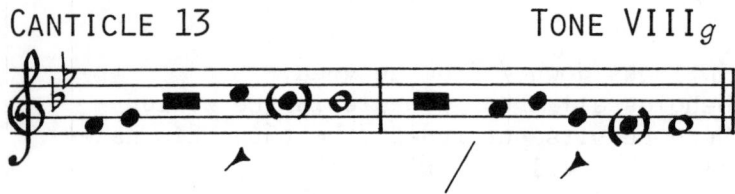

1 *Glo - ry* to you, Lord God of our fá-thers;*
   you are worthy of praise; / glo-ry tó you.
2 Glory to you for the radiance of your hó-ly Name;*
   we will praise you and highly exalt / you for év-er.

REFRAIN

3 *Glo - ry* to you in the splendor of your tém-ple;*
   on the throne of your majesty, / glo-ry tó you.
4 Glory to you, seated between the Chér-u-bim;*
   we will praise you and highly exalt / you for év-er.

REFRAIN

5 *Glo - ry* to you, beholding the dépths;*
   in the high vault of heaven, / glo-ry tó you.
6 Glory to you, Father, Son, and Holy Spír-it;*
   we will praise you and highly exalt / you for év-er.

REFRAIN

VIGIL OF PENTECOST ABC *(or Early Service)*

REFRAIN

With the Lord there is mer-cy; with him there

is plen-te-ous re - demp - tion.

PSALM 130   TONE IIIb

1 *Out of* the depths have I called to you, O LORD;
   LÓRD, hear mÿ voice;*
       let your ears consider well the voice of
                         my sup - / pli-cá-tion.

                                                    REFRAIN

2 *If yöu*, LORD, were to note whát is dóne ä-miss,*
       O Lord, / who cóuld stand?
3 For there is for-gíve-ness wïth you;*
       therefore / you sháll be feared.

                                                    REFRAIN

4 *I wait* for the LORD; my sóul waits för him;*
       in his word / is mÿ hope.
5 My soul waits for the LORD,
   more than watchmen fór the mórn-ing,*
       more than watchmen for / the mórn-ing.

                                                    REFRAIN

6 *O Is* - rael, wáit for thë LORD,*
       for with the LORD there / is mér-cy;*
7 With him there is plente-oús re-dëmp-tion,*
       and he shall redeem Israel / from áll their sins.

                                                    REFRAIN
                                                    BCP, p. 784

VIGIL OF PENTECOST ABC   *(or Early Service)*

REFRAIN

You shall draw wa-ter with re - joic-ing

from the springs of sal-va - tion.

CANTICLE 9   TONE VIIIg

1 *Sure - ly*, it is God who sáves me;*
   I will trust in him and / not be á-fraid.
2 For the Lord is my stronghold and my súre de-fense,*
   and he will / be my Sáv-ior.

                                        REFRAIN

4 *And on* that day you shall sáy,*
   Give thanks to the Lord and / call up-ón his Name;
5 Make his deeds known among the péo-ples;*
   see that they remember that his Name / is ex-ált-ed.

                                        REFRAIN

6 *Sing the* praises of the Lord, for he has done
                              gréat things,*
   and this is / known in áll the world.
7 Cry aloud, inhabitants of Zion, ring out your jóy,*
   for the great one in the midst of you is
                              the Holy / One of Iś-ra-el.

                                        REFRAIN

Vigil of Pentecost ABC *(or Early Service)*

Refrain

Send forth your Spir-it, O Lord,

and re - new the face of the earth.

Alternate Refrain   Alleluia VIII

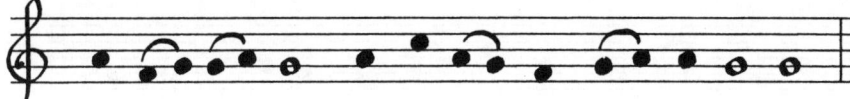

Hal-le - lu - jah, hal-le-lu - jah, hal - le-lu-jah!

Psalm 104   Tone VIII*g*

25 *O LORD,* how manifold are your wórks!*
    in wisdom you have made them all;
    the earth is full / of your créa-tures.
26 Yonder is the great and wide sea
    with its living things too many to núm-ber,*
    crea - / tures both smáll and great.

REFRAIN

28 *All of* them loók to you*
    to give them their food / in due séa-son.
29 You give it to them; they gáth-er it;*
    you open your hand, and they are / filled with
    goód things.

REFRAIN

(continued)

BCP, p. 736

REFRAIN

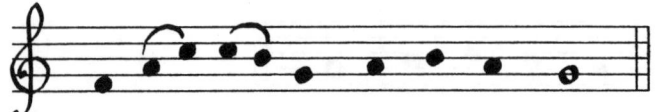

Send forth your Spir-it, O Lord,

and re - new the face of the earth.

ALTERNATE REFRAIN   ALLELUIA VIII

Hal-le - lu - jah, hal-le-lu - jah, hal - le-lu-jah!

PSALM 104   TONE VIIIg

30 *You hide* your face, and they are tér-ri-fied;*
   you take away their breath,
   and they die and re - / turn to théir dust.
31 You send forth your Spirit, and they are cre-á-ted;*
   and so you renew the / face of thé earth.

                                          REFRAIN

32 *May the* glory of the LORD endure for év-er;*
   may the LORD re - / joice in áll his works.
35 May these words of mine pleáse him;*
   I will re - / joice in thé LORD.

                                          REFRAIN

Vigil of Pentecost ABC *(or Early Service)*

Alleluia II

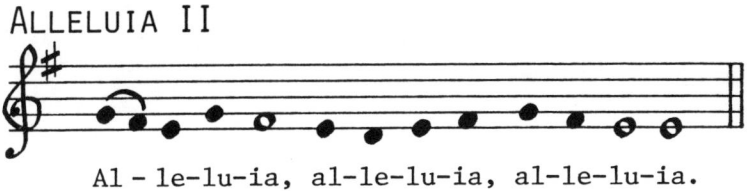

Al - le-lu-ia, al-le-lu-ia, al-le-lu-ia.

Verse   Tone II

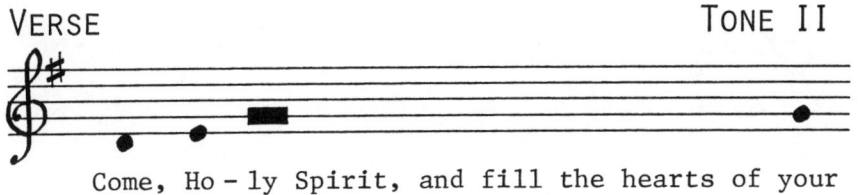

Come, Ho - ly Spirit, and fill the hearts of your

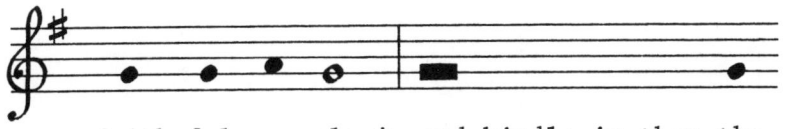

faith-ful peo-ple,* and kindle in them the

fire of your love.

THE DAY OF PENTECOST C — *Principal Service*

REFRAIN

Send forth your Spir-it, O Lord,

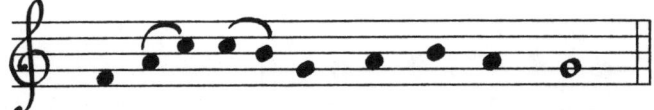

and re - new the face of the earth.

ALTERNATE REFRAIN   ALLELUIA VIII

Hal-le - lu - jah, hal-le-lu - jah, hal - le-lu-jah!

PSALM 104   TONE VIIIg

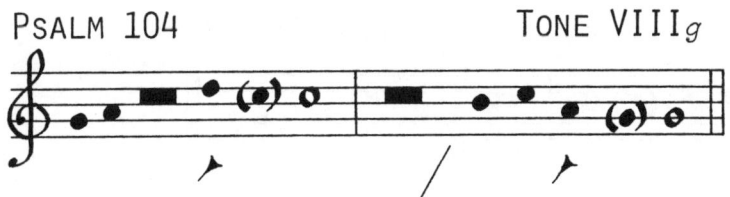

25 *O LORD*, how manifold are your wórks!*
    in wisdom you have made them all;
    the earth is full / of your créa-tures.
26 Yonder is the great and wide sea
    with its living things too many to núm-ber,*
    crea - / tures both smáll and great.

REFRAIN

28 *All of* them loók to you*
    to give them their food / in due séa-son.
29 You give it to them; they gáth-er it;*
    you open your hand, and they are / filled with
          góod things.

REFRAIN

(continued)

BCP, p. 736

REFRAIN

Send forth your Spir-it, O Lord,

and re - new the face of the earth.

ALTERNATE REFRAIN   ALLELUIA VIII

Hal-le - lu - jah, hal-le-lu - jah, hal - le-lu-jah!

PSALM 104   TONE VIII*g*

30 *You hide* your face, and they are tér-ri-fied;*
    you take away their breath,
    and they die and re - / turn to théir dust.
31 You send forth your Spirit, and they are cre-á-ted;*
    and so you renew the / face of thé earth.

                                        REFRAIN

32 *May the* glory of the LORD endure for év-er;*
    may the LORD re - / joice in áll his works.
35 May these words of mine pleáse him;*
    I will re - / joice in thé LORD.

                                        REFRAIN

REFRAIN

Hap-py is the na-tion whose God is the Lord.

PSALM 33   TONE Va

13 *The LORD* looks down from héav-en,*
       and beholds all the péo-ple ín the world.
14 From where he sits enthroned he túrns his gaze*
       on all who dwéll on thé earth.

                                      REFRAIN

15 *He fash* - ions all the héarts of them*
       and un-der-stánds all théir works.
18 Behold, the eye of the LORD is upon those who
                  féar him,*
       on those who wáit up-ón his love,

                                      REFRAIN

19 *To pluck* their líves from death,*
       and to feed them in tíme of fám-ine.
20 Our soul waits for the LÓRD;*
       he is our hélp and oúr shield.

                                      REFRAIN

21 *In - deed,* our heart rejoices in hím,*
       for in his holy Náme we pút our trust.
22 Let your loving-kindness, O LORD, be up-ón us,*
       as we have pút our trúst in you.

                                      REFRAIN

ALLELUIA II

Al - le-lu-ia, al-le-lu-ia, al-le-lu-ia.

VERSE   TONE II

Come, Ho - ly Spirit, and fill the hearts of your

faith-ful peo-ple,* and kindle in them the

fire of your love.

TRINITY SUNDAY C

REFRAIN

Glo-ry to you, Fa-ther, Son, and Ho-ly Spir-it.

CANTICLE 2   TONE VIII*g*

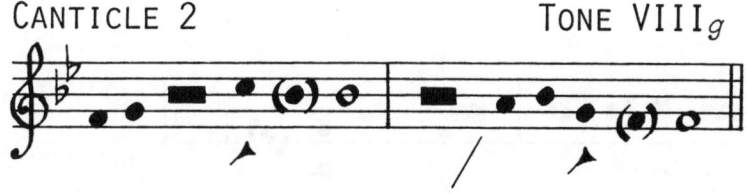

1 *Bless - ed* art thou, O Lord God of our fá-thers;*
     praised and exalted above / all for év-er.
2 Blessed art thou for the Name of thy Má-jes-ty;*
     praised and exalted above / all for év-er.

REFRAIN

3 *Bless - ed* art thou in the temple of thy hó-li-ness;*
     praised and exalted above / all for év-er.
4 Blessed art thou that beholdest the depths,
   and dwellest between the Chér-u-bim;*
     praised and exalted above / all for év-er.
5 Blessed art thou on the glorious throne of thy
                    kíng-dom;*
     praised and exalted above / all for év-er.

REFRAIN

6 *Bless - ed* art thou in the firmament of heáv-en;*
     praised and exalted above / all for év-er.
7 Blessed art thou, O Father, Son, and Holy Spír-it;*
     praised and exalted above / all for év-er.

REFRAIN

TRINITY SUNDAY C

REFRAIN

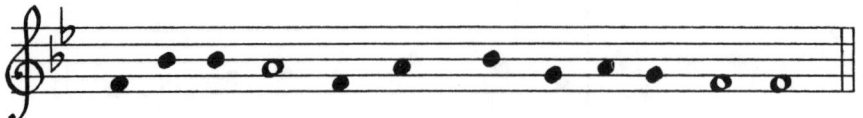

Glo-ry to you, Fa-ther, Son and Ho-ly Spir-it.

CANTICLE 13   TONE VIIIg

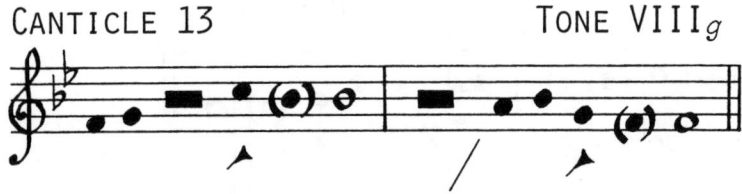

1 *Glo - ry* to you, Lord God of our fá-thers;*
   you are worthy of praise; / glo-ry tó you.
2 Glory to you for the radiance of your hó-ly Name;*
   we will praise you and highly exalt / you for év-er.

                                        REFRAIN

3 *Glo - ry* to you in the splendor of your tém-ple;*
   on the throne of your majesty, / glo-ry tó you.
4 Glory to you, seated between the Chér-u-bim;*
   we will praise you and highly exalt / you for év-er.

                                        REFRAIN

5 *Glo - ry* to you, beholding the depths;*
   in the high vault of heaven, / glo-ry tó you.
6 Glory to you, Father, Son, and Holy Spír-it;*
   we will praise you and highly exalt / you for év-er.

                                        REFRAIN

BCP, p. 90

TRINITY SUNDAY C

REFRAIN

As-cribe to the Lord the glo - ry due his Name.

PSALM 29   TONE IV*a*

3 *The voïce* of the LORD is upon the waters;
    the God of / glo-ry thún-ders;*
      the LORD is upon / the might-y wá-ters.
4 The voice of the LORD is a pow - / er-ful voíce;*
      the voice of the LORD is / a voice of splén-dor.
5 The voice of the LORD / breaks the cé-dar trees;*
      the LORD breaks the / ce-dars of Lé-ba-non;

REFRAIN

6 *He makes* Lebanon skip / like a cálf,*
      and Mount Hermon / like a young wíld ox.
7 The voice of the LORD splits the flames of fire;
      the voice of the LORD / shakes the wíl-der-ness;*
        the LORD shakes the wil - / der-ness of Ká-desh.
8 The voice of the LORD / makes the oák trees writhe*
      —— / and strips the fór-ests bare.

REFRAIN

9 *And in* the temple / of the LÓRD*
      all / are cry-ing, "Gló-ry!"
10 The LORD sits en - / throned a-bóve the flood;*
      the LORD sits enthroned / as King for év-er-more.
11 The LORD shall give strength / to his péo-ple;*
      the LORD shall give his people / the bless-ing
             óf peace.

REFRAIN

TRINITY SUNDAY C

ALLELUIA VIII

Al-le – lu – ia, al-le-lu – ia, al – le-lu-ia.

VERSE (Rev. 1:4)   TONE VIIIg

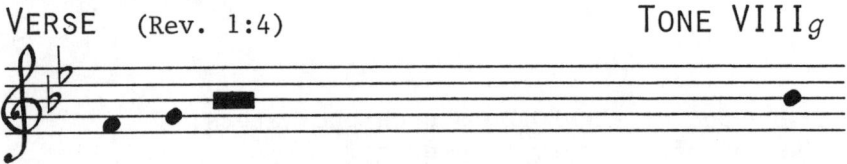

Glo – ry to the Father and to the Son and to the

Ho-ly Spir-it;* to God who is, and who was,

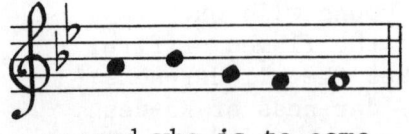

and who is to come.

Proper 1 C

Same as 6 Epiphany C

Proper 2 C

Same as 7 Epiphany C

Proper 3 C

Same as 8 Epiphany C

REFRAIN

Sing to the Lord a new song; sing to the

Lord, all the whole earth.

PSALM 96   TONE VI

2 *Sing to* the LORD / and bléss his Name;*
   proclaim the good news of his salva - / tion
                          fröm dáy to day.
3 Declare his glory among / the ná-tions*
   and his wonders a - / mong äll péo-ples.

                                        REFRAIN

4 *For great* is the LORD and great - / ly tó be praised;*
   he is more to be / feared thän áll gods.
5 As for all the gods of the nations, they are / but
                          í-dols;*
   but it is the LORD who / made thë héav-ens.

                                        REFRAIN

6 *Oh, the* majesty and the magnificence of / his prés-ence!*
   Oh, the power and the splendor of his / sanc-tü-ár-y!
7 Ascribe to the LORD, you families of / the péo-ples;*
   ascribe to the LORD hon - / or añd pów-er.

                                        REFRAIN

(continued)

PROPER 4 C *(continuation)*

REFRAIN

Sing to the Lord a new   song;   sing to the

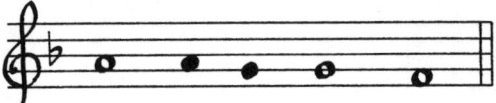

Lord, all the whole earth.

PSALM 96   TONE VI

8 *As - cribe* to the LORD the hon - / or dúe his Name;*
   bring offerings and / come ïn-tó his courts.
9 Worship the LORD in the beauty / of hó-li-ness;*
   let the whole earth trem - / ble bë-fóre him.

REFRAIN

ALLELUIA - Ad libitum

BCP, p. 725

PROPER 5 C

REFRAIN

O   Lord my God, I cried out to you,

and you re-stored me to health.

PSALM 30   TONE I*f*

1   *I will* exalt you, O LORD,
    because you have líft-ed mé up*
        and have not let my enemies / tri-umph ö-ver më.
3   You brought me up, O LÓRD, from thé dead;*
        you restored my life as I was go - / ing down
                to the gräve.

                                            REFRAIN

4   *Sing to* the LORD, you sér-vants óf his;*
        give thanks for the remembrance / of his hö-li-nëss.
5   For his wrath endures but the twin-kling óf an eye,*
        his favor / for a life-time.
6   —— Weep-ing may spénd the night,*
        but joy comes / in the mörn-ing.

                                            REFRAIN

12 *You have* turned my wailing ín-to danc-ing;*
        you have put off my sack cloth / and clothed
                më with jöy.
13 Therefore my heart sings to you with-out céas-ing;*
        O LORD my God, I will give you / thanks for év-er.

                                            REFRAIN

ALLELUIA - Ad libitum   *BCP, p. 621*

PROPER 6 C

REFRAIN

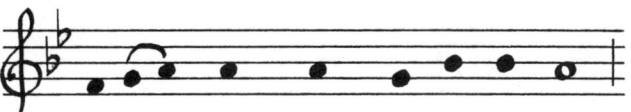

I ac - know-ledged my sin to you,

and you for-gave me the guilt of my sin.

PSALM 32   TONE IIIb

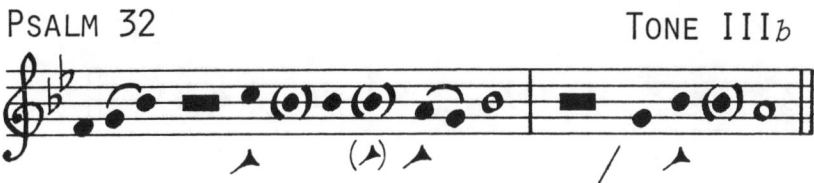

1 *Hap - py* are they whose transgressions are for-gív-en,*
   and whose sin / is pút a-way!
2 Happy are they to whom the LORD im-pútes no guilt,*
   and in whose spirit / there is no guile!

REFRAIN

3 *While I* held my tongue, my bones with-ered a-way,*
   because of my groan - / ing áll day long.
4 For your hand was heavy up-ón me dáy and night;*
   my moisture was dried up as in the heat / of súm-mer.

REFRAIN

5 *Then I* ac-know-ledged my sín to you,*
   and did not / con-céal my guilt.
6 I said, "I will confess my trans-grés-sions tó
                  thë LORD."*
   Then you forgave me the guilt / of mý sin.

REFRAIN

(continued)

PROPER 6 C *(continuation)*

REFRAIN

I ac - know-ledged my sin to you,

and you for-gave me the guilt of my sin.

PSALM 32   TONE IIIb

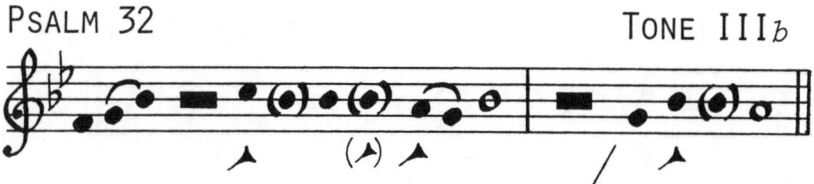

7 *There - főre* all the faithful will make their prayers
            to you in time of trőu-ble;*
    when the great waters overflow, they shall / not
            reách them.
8 You are my hiding place;
    you pre-sérve me from trőu-ble;*
        you surround me with shouts of / de-lív-er-ance.

                                    REFRAIN

ALLELUIA - Ad libitum

PROPER 7 C

REFRAIN

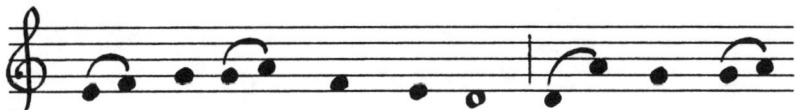

Lord, my soul clings to you; your right hand

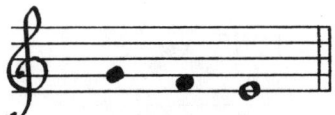

holds me fast.

PSALM 63   TONE IVe

1 *O God*, you are my God; eager - / ly I séek you;*
    my soul thirsts for you, my flesh faints for you,
    as in a barren and dry land where / there is nö wä-ter.
2 Therefore I have gazed upon you / in your hó-ly place,*
    that I might behold your pow - / er and yöur gló-ry.

                                        REFRAIN

3 *For your* loving-kindness is bet - / ter than
                    life it-self;*
    my / lips shall give yöu praise.
4 So will I bless you as long / as I líve*
    and lift up / my hands iñ yöur Name.

                                        REFRAIN

5 *My soul* is content, as with mar - / row and fát-ness,*
    and my mouth prais - / es you with jöy-fül lips,
7 For you have / been my hélp-er,*
    and under the shadow of / your wings Ï wíll
                    rë-joice.
                                        REFRAIN

ALLELUIA - Ad libitum

                                        BCP, p. 670

PROPER 8 C

REFRAIN

The Lord will show me the path of life.

PSALM 16　　　　　　　　　TONE V𝑎

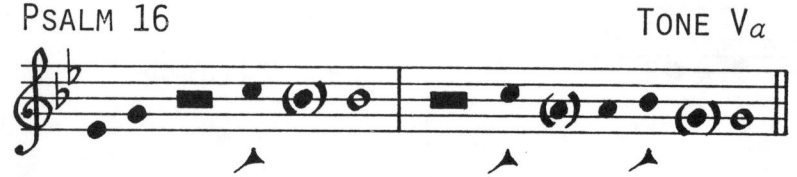

5　*O LORD*, you are my portion and my cúp;*
　　it is yóu who up-hóld my lot.
6　My boundaries enclose a pléas-ant land;*
　　indeed, I have a góod-ly hér-i-tage.

REFRAIN

7　*I will* bless the LORD who gives me cóun-sel;*
　　my heart teaches me, níght af-tér night.
8　I have set the LORD always be-fóre me;*
　　because he is at my right hand Í shall nót fall.

REFRAIN

9　*My heart*, therefore, is glad, and my spirit re-jóic-es;*
　　my body al-só shall rést in hope.
10　For you will not abandon me to the gráve,*
　　nor let your hó-ly one sée the Pit.

REFRAIN

11　*You will* show me the páth of life;*
　　in your presence there is fullness of joy,
　　and in your right hand are pléas-ures for év-er-more.

REFRAIN

ALLELUIA - Ad libitum

PROPER 9 C

REFRAIN

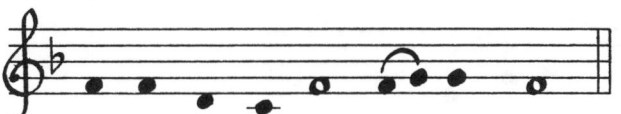

Be joy-ful in God, all you lands.

PSALM 66   TONE VI

1b *Sing the* glory / of his Name;*
    sing the / glo-ry of his praise.
2 Say to God, "How awesome / are your deeds!*
    because of your great strength your enemies / cringe
             bë-fóre you.

                                    REFRAIN

3 *All the* earth bows down / be-fóre you,*
    sings to you, / sings öut yóur Name."
4 Come now and see / the wórks of God,*
    how wonderful he is in his doing / toward äll péo-ple.

                                      REFRAIN

5 *He turned* the sea into dry land,
    so that they went through the wa - / ter ón foot,*
    and there / we rë-joíced in him.
6 In his might he rules for ever;
    his eyes keep watch over / the ná-tions;*
    let no rebel rise / up ä-gaínst him.

                                      REFRAIN

7 *Bless our* God, / you péo-ples;*
    make the voice of his / praise tö bé heard;
8 Who holds / our soúls in life,*
    and will not al - / low öur feét to slip.

                                      REFRAIN

ALLELUIA - Ad libitum

Proper 10 C

Refrain

Lead me in your truth and teach me,

for you are the God of my sal-va-tion.

Psalm 25   Tone VIIb

3 *Shŏw mē* your wáys, Ó LORD,*
   and teách me yóur paths.
5 Remember, O LORD, your com-pás-sion añd love,*
   for they are from év-er-lást-ing.

REFRAIN

6 *Rĕ - mĕm* - ber not the sins of my youth and
                    mý trans-grés-sions;*
   remember me according to your love
   and for the sake of your goód-ness, Ó LORD.
7 Gracious and úp-right ís the LORD;*
   therefore he teaches sín-ners ín his way.

REFRAIN

8 *Hĕ guĭdes* the húm-ble in dó-ing right*
   and teaches his wáy to the lów-ly.
9 All the paths of the LORD are lóve and faíth-ful-ness*
   to those who keep his covenant and his
                    tés-ti-mó-nies.

REFRAIN

ALLELUIA - Ad libitum

PROPER 11 C

REFRAIN

The right-eous shall a-bide up-on God's ho-ly hill.

PSALM 15   TONE VIII*g*

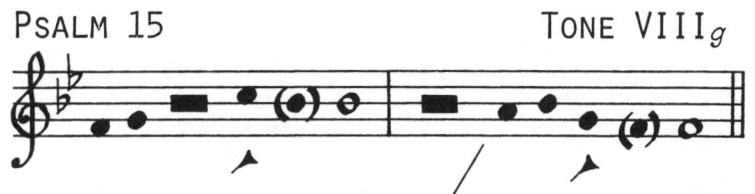

1 *LORD, who* may dwell in your ta-ber-ná-cle?*
   who may abide up – / on your hó-ly hill?
2 Whoever leads a blameless life and does what is ríght,*
   who speaks the / truth from hís heart.

REFRAIN

3 *There is* no guile upon his tongue;
   he does no evil to his friénd;*
   he does not heap contempt up – / on his neígh-bor.
4 In his sight the wicked is re-jéct-ed,*
   but he honors / those who feár the LORD.

REFRAIN

5 *He has* sworn to do nó wrong*
   and does / not take báck his word.
6 He does not give his money in hópe of gain,*
   nor does he take a bribe a – / gainst the ín-no-cent.

REFRAIN

7 *Who – ev –* er does thése things*
   shall nev – / er be ó-ver-thrown.

REFRAIN

ALLELUIA – Ad libitum

BCP, p. 599

PROPER 12 C

REFRAIN

When I called, you an - swered me;

O Lord, your love en-dures for ev-er.

PSALM 138   TONE I_g

1 *I will* give thanks to you, O LORD, with my whole
                     heart;*
   before the gods / I will sing your praise.
2 I will bow down toward your holy tém-ple
   and práise your Name,*
       because of your / love and faíth-ful-ness.

                                    REFRAIN

3 *For you* have gló-ri-fíed your Name*
       and your / word a-bóve all things.
4 When I cálled, you án-swered me;*
       you increased my / strength with-ín me.

                                    REFRAIN

7 *Though the* LORD be high, he cáres for the lów-ly;*
       he perceives the / haugh-ty fróm a-far.
8 Though I walk in the midst of tróu-ble, you kéep
                     me safe;*
       you stretch forth your hand against the fury of
                     my enemies;
       your right / hand shall sáve me.

                                    REFRAIN

(continued)   *BCP, p. 793*

PROPER 12 C   *(continuation)*

REFRAIN

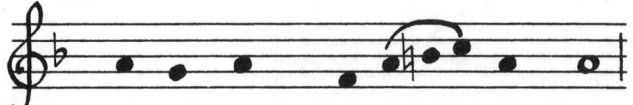

When I called, you an - swered me;

O Lord, your love en-dures for ev-er.

PSALM 138   TONE I*g*

9 *The LORD* will make good his púr-pose fór me;*
    O LORD, your love endures for ever;
    do not abandon the / works of yöür hands.

REFRAIN

ALLELUIA - Ad libitum

PROPER 13 C

REFRAIN

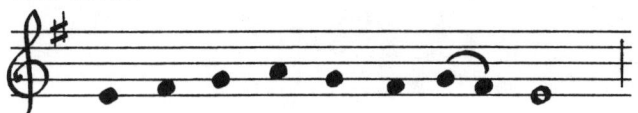

We can nev-er ran-som our-selves,

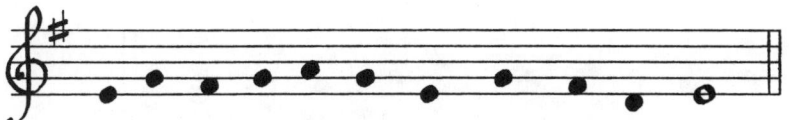

or de-liv-er to God the price of our life.

PSALM 49   TONE II

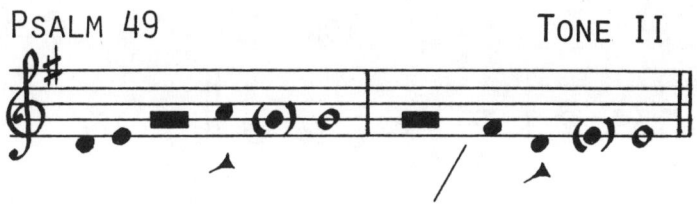

1 *Hear this*, all you peoples;
    hearken, all you who dwell in the wórld,*
        you of high degree and low, rich and
                        poor / to-géth-er.
2 My mouth shall speak of wís-dom,*
        and my heart shall meditate on un - / der-stánd-ing.

                                    REFRAIN

4 *Why should* I be afraid in é-vil days,*
        when the wickedness of those at my
                        heels / sur-roúnds me,
5 The wickedness of those who put their trust
                        in their goóds,*
        and boast of their / great rích-es?

                                    REFRAIN

7 *For the* ransom of our life is so gréat,*
        that we should never have enough / to páy it,
8 In order to live for ever and év-er,*
        and nev - / er sée the grave.

                                    REFRAIN

(continued)

BCP, p. 652

REFRAIN

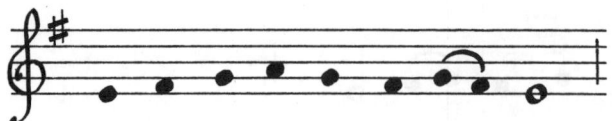

We can nev-er ran-som our-selves,

or de-liv-er to God the price of our life.

PSALM 49   TONE II

9 *For we* see that the wise die also;
   like the dull and stupid they pér-ish*
   and leave their wealth to those
                    who / come áf-ter them.
10 Even though honored, they cannot live for év-er;*
   they are like the beasts / that pér-ish.

                                        REFRAIN

ALLELUIA - Ad libitum

PROPER 14 C

REFRAIN

Our soul waits for the Lord;

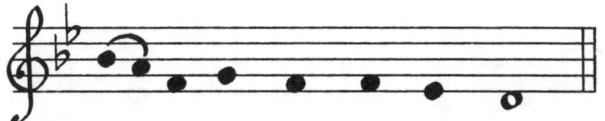

he is our help and our shield.

PSALM 33   TONE III♭

13 *The LÖRD* looks down from heäv-en,*
      and beholds all the peo - / ple in the world.
14 From where he sits en-thróned he turns his gaze*
      on all who / dwell ón the earth.

                                            REFRAIN

18 *Be - hold,* the eye of the LORD is upon thóse
                        who feär him,*
      on those who wait / up-ón his love,
19 To plúck their líves fröm death,*
      and to feed them in time / of fám-ine.

                                            REFRAIN

21 *In - deed,* our heart re-joíc-es in him,*
      for in his holy Name / we pút our trust.
22 Let your loving-kindness, O LÓRD, be up-ön us,*
      as we have put / our trúst in you.

                                            REFRAIN

ALLELUIA - Ad libitum

PROPER 15 C

REFRAIN

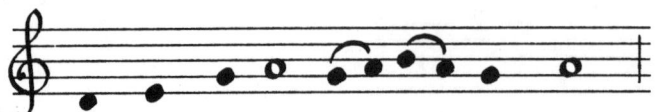

A-rise, O God, and rule the earth,

for you shall take all na-tions for your own.

PSALM 82   TONE IVa

1 *God takes* his stand in the coun - / cil of héav-en;*
    he gives judgment in / the midst of thé gods:
2 "How long will you / judge un-júst-ly,*
    and show fa - / vor to the wíck-ed?
                                 REFRAIN

4 *Res - cue* the weak / and the póor;*
    deliver them from the pow - / er of the wíck-ed.
5 They do not know, neither do they understand;
    they go a - / bout in dárk-ness;*
    all the foundations of / the earth are shák-en.
                                   REFRAIN

6 *Now I* say to you, / 'You are góds,*
    and all of you chil - / dren of the Móst High;
7 Nevertheless, you shall / die like mór-tals,*
    —— / and fall like án-y prince.'"
                                   REFRAIN

ALLELUIA - Ad libitum

PROPER 16 C

REFRAIN

The Lord of hosts is with us;

the God of Ja-cob is our strong-hold.

PSALM 46   TONE V*a*

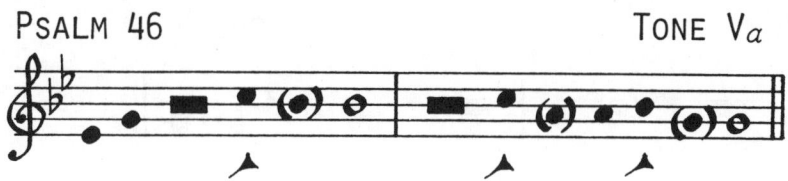

1 *God is* our refuge and strĕngth,*
      a very present hĕlp in trŏu-ble.
2 Therefore we will not fear, though the eărth
                  be moved,*
      and though the mountains be toppled into the
                  dĕpths of thĕ sea;
3 Though its waters răge and foam,*
      and though the mountains tremble ăt its tŭ-mult.

                                    REFRAIN

5 *There is* a river whose streams make glad the
                  city of Gŏd,*
      the holy habitation ŏf the Mŏst High.
6 God is in the midst of her;
      she shall not be ŏ-ver-thrown;*
      God shall help her ăt the brĕak of day.
7 The nations make much ado, and the kingdoms
                  are shăk-en;*
      God has spoken, and the eărth shall mĕlt a-way.

                                    REFRAIN

(continued)

PROPER 16 C   *(continuation)*

REFRAIN

The Lord of hosts is with us;

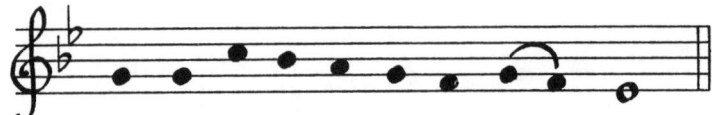

the God of Ja-cob is our strong-hold.

PSALM 46   TONE Va

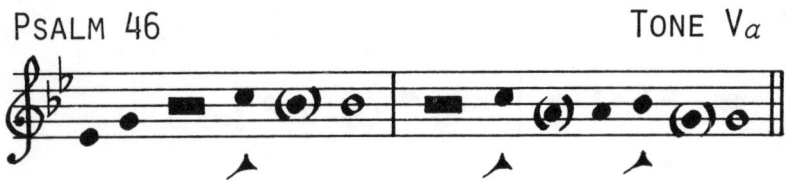

9   *Come now* and look upon the works of the LORD,*
        what awesome things hé has dóne on earth.
10 It is he who makes war to cease in áll the world;*
        he breaks the bow, and shatters the spear,
        and búrns the shíelds with fire.
11 "Be still, then, and know that Í am God;*
        I will be exalted among the nations;
        I will be ex-ált-ed ín the earth.

                                    REFRAIN

ALLELUIA - Ad libitum

PROPER 17 C

REFRAIN

Hap-py are they who fear the Lord.

PSALM 112   TONE VI

2 *Their de̎* - scendants will be might - / ˌˌy ín the land;*
      the generation of the up -/ right will bé blessed.
3 Wealth and riches will be / in théir house,*
      and their righteousness will / last för év-er.

                                              REFRAIN

4 *Light shi̎nes* in the darkness for / the úp-right;*
      the righteous are merciful and full / of cöm-pás-sion.
5 It is good for them to be generous / in lénd-ing*
      and to manage their af - / fairs wïth jús-tice.

                                              REFRAIN

6 *For the̎y* will never / be shák-en;*
      the righteous will be kept in everlast - / ing
                    rë-mém-brance.
7 They will not be afraid of any e - / vil rú-mors;*
      their heart is right;
      they put / their trüst ín the LORD.

                                              REFRAIN

9 *They ha̎ve* given free - / ly tó the poor,*
      and their righteousness stands fast for ever;
      they will hold up their / head wïth hón-or.

                                              REFRAIN

ALLELUIA - Ad libitum

PROPER 18 C

REFRAIN

Hap-py are they whose de-light is in the

law of the Lord.

PSALM 1   TONE VIIb

1 *Hap - pÿ* are they who have not walked in the counsel
óf the wíck-ed,*
   nor lingered in the way of sinners,
   nor sat in the séats of the scórn-ful!
2 Their delight is in the láw of thé LORD,*
   and they meditate on his láw day ańd night.

                                REFRAIN

3 *Theÿ aŕe* like trees planted by streams of water,
   bearing fruit in due season, with leaves that
                 dó not wíth-er;*
   everything they dó shall prós-per.
4 It is not so wíth the wíck-ed;*
   they are like chaff which the wínd blows á-way.

                                  REFRAIN

5 *Theŕe - foŕe* the wicked shall not stand úp-right
             when júdg-ment comes,*
   nor the sinner in the council óf the ríght-eous.
6 For the LORD knows the wáy of the ríght-eous,*
   but the way of the wíck-ed ís doomed.

                                  REFRAIN

ALLELUIA - Ad libitum   *BCP, p. 585*

PROPER 19 C

REFRAIN

Cre-ate in me a clean heart, O God.

PSALM 51   TONE VIIIc

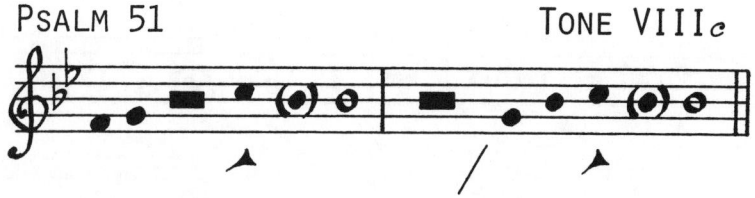

1 *Have mer* - cy on me, O God, according to your
                    loving-kínd-ness;*
   in your great compassion blot out / my of-féns-es.
2 Wash me through and through from my wíck-ed-ness*
   and / cleanse me fróm my sin.

                                    REFRAIN

3 *For I* know my trans-grés-sions,*
   and my sin is ev - / er be-fóre me.
4 Against you only have I sinńed*
   and done what is / e-vil ín your sight.

                                    REFRAIN

7 *For be* - hold, you look for truth deep with-ín me,*
   and will make me understand / wis-dom sé-cret-ly.
8 Purge me from my sin, and I shall be púre;*
   wash me, and I / shall be cleán in-deed.

                                    REFRAIN

ALLELUIA - Ad libitum

PROPER 20 C

REFRAIN

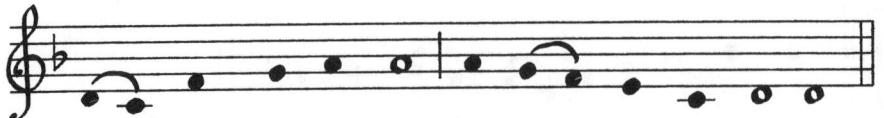

Give thanks to the Lord who cares for the low-ly.

PSALM 138   TONE I*f*

1 *I will* give thanks to you, O LORD, with my whóle heart;*
   before the gods / I will síng your praise.
2 I will bow down toward your holy tém-ple
  and práise your Name,*
   because of your / love and faíth-ful-nèss;

                                 REFRAIN

4 *When I* —— cálled, you án-swered me;*
   you increased my / strength with-ín me.
7 Though the LORD be high, he cáres for the lów-ly;*
   he perceives the / haugh-ty fróm a-fär.

                                   REFRAIN

8 *Though I* walk in the midst of tróu-ble, you keép
                me safe;*
  you stretch forth your hand against the fury of
              my enemies;
  your right / hand shall sáve mè.
9 The LORD will make good his púr-pose fór me;*
   O LORD, your love endures for ever;
   do not abandon the / works of yöür hànds.

                                   REFRAIN

ALLELUIA - Ad libitum

PROPER 21 C

REFRAIN

Praise the Lord, O my soul.

PSALM 146   TONE II

4 *Hap-py* are they who have the God of Jacob for
                their hélp!*
    whose hope is in the / LORD théir God;
5 Who made heaven and earth, the seas, and all
                that is ín them;*
    who keeps his promise / for év-er;

                                REFRAIN

6 *Who gives* justice to those who are op-preśsed,*
    and food to those / who hún-ger.
7 The LORD sets the prisoners free;
    the LORD opens the eyes of the blínd;*
        the LORD lifts up those who / are bowed down;

                                REFRAIN

8 *The LORD* loves the righteous;
    the LORD cares for the strán-ger;*
        he sustains the orphan and widow,
        but frustrates the way of / the wíck-ed.
9 The LORD shall reign for év-er,*
    your God, O Zion, throughout all generations.
    Hal - / le-lú-jah!

                                REFRAIN

ALLELUIA - Ad libitum

BCP, p. 803

PROPER 22 C

REFRAIN

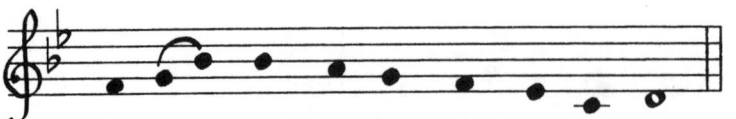

Put your trust in the Lord and do good.

PSALM 37   TONE IIIb

1 *Do nöt* fret yourself because of é-vil do̊-ers,*
     do not be jealous of those / who dó wrong.
3 Put your trust in the LÓRD and do̊ good;*
     dwell in the land and feed on / its rích-es.

                                              REFRAIN

4 *Take dë - —— líght in the LORD,*
     and he shall give you / your heárt's de-sire.
5 Commit your way to the LORD and pút your trúst in him,*
     and he will bring / it tó pass.

                                              REFRAIN

6 *He wiłł* make your righteousness as cleár as the light*
     and your just dealing as / the noón-day.
7 Be still be-fóre thë LORD*
     and wait pa - / tient-lý for him.

                                              REFRAIN

8 *Do nöt* fret yourself over the óne who prös-pers,*
     the one who succeeds / in é-vil schemes.
10 For evildoers sháll be ćut off,*
     but those who wait upon the LORD shall / pos-séss
                           the land.

                                              REFRAIN

ALLELUIA - Ad libitum

                                              BCP, p. 633

PROPER 23 C

REFRAIN

Let the Name of the Lord be praised from

this time forth for ev-er-more.

PSALM 113   TONE IVe

1 *Hal - lë - lujah!*
   Give praise, you / ser-vants óf the LORD;*
      praise / the Name öf the LORD.
4 The LORD is high a - / bove all ná-tions,*
      and his glory / a-bove thë héäv-ens.

                                        REFRAIN

5 *Who is* like the LORD our God, who / sits en-thróned
                           on high,*
      but stoops to behold / the heav-ens ańd thë earth?
6 He takes up the weak out / of the dúst*
      and lifts up the / poor from thë ásh-es.

                                        REFRAIN

7 *He sets* them / with the prínc-es,*
      with the princ - / es of his péö-ple.
8 He makes the woman / of a chíld-less house*
      to be a joyful / moth-er öf chíl-dren.

                                        REFRAIN

ALLELUIA - Ad libitum

PROPER 24 C

REFRAIN

My help comes from the Lord,

the mak-er of heav-en and earth.

PSALM 121   TONE V*a*

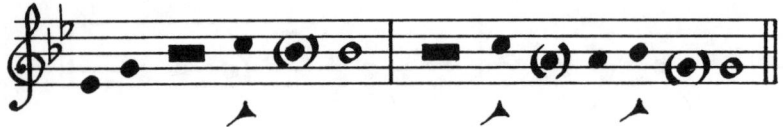

1 *I lift* up my eyes to the hílls;*
      from whére is my hélp to come?
2 My help comes from the LÓRD,*
      the maker of héav-en añd earth.   REFRAIN

3 *He will* not let your fóot be moved*
      and he who watches over you wíll not fáll a-sleep.
4 Behold, he who keeps watch over Iś-ra-el*
      shall neither slúm-ber nór sleep;   REFRAIN

5 *The LORD* himself watches ó-ver you;*
      the LORD is your sháde at your ríght hand,
6 So that the sun shall not strike you by dáy,*
      —— nór the moón by night.   REFRAIN

7 *The LORD* shall preserve you from all é-vil;*
      it is hé who shall keép you safe.
8 The LORD shall watch over your going out and
                        your cóm-ing in,*
      from this time fórth for év-er-more.   REFRAIN

ALLELUIA - Ad libitum   *BCP, p. 779*

PROPER 25 C

REFRAIN

O Lord of hosts, hap-py are they who

put their trust in you.

PSALM 84   TONE VI

1 *How dear* to me is your dwelling, / O LORD of hosts!*
   My soul has a desire and longing for the courts of
                    the LORD;
      my heart and my flesh rejoice / in thë lív-ing God.
2 The sparrow has found her a house
   and the swallow a nest where she / may láy her young;*
      by the side of your altars, O LORD of hosts,
      / my Kïng añd my God.

                                        REFRAIN

3 *Hap - py* are they who dwell / in yóur house!*
      they will al - / ways bë práis-ing you.
4 Happy are the people whose strength / is ín you!*
      whose hearts are set / on thë píl-grims' way.

                                        REFRAIN

5 *Those who* go through the desolate valley will find
                    it / a pláce of springs,*
      for the early rains have covered it with / pools
                    öf wá-ter.
6 They will climb / from height to height,*
      and the God of gods will reveal him - / self ïn Zí-on.

                                        REFRAIN

ALLELUIA - Ad libitum   *BCP, p. 707*

PROPER 26 C

REFRAIN

I ac-knowl-edged my sin to you,

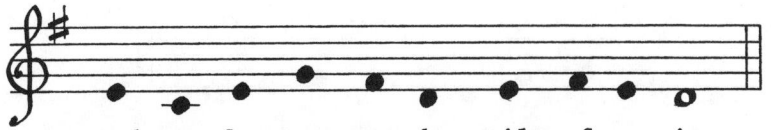

and you for-gave me the guilt of my sin.

PSALM 32   TONE VIIb

1 *Hap-py* are they whose transgressions are for-gív-en,*
   and whose sín is pút a-way!
2 Happy are they to whom the LÓRD im-pútes no guilt,*
   and in whose spirit thére is nó guile!

                                        REFRAIN

3 *While I* held my tongue, my bones wíth-ered á-way,*
   because of my gróan-ing áll day long.
4 For your hand was heavy up-ón me dáy and night;*
   my moisture was dried up as in the héat of súm-mer.

                                        REFRAIN

5 *Then I* ac-knówl-edged my sín to you,*
   and did nót con-céal my guilt.
6 I said, "I will confess my trans-grés-sions tó
                  the LORD."*
   Then you forgave me the gúilt of mý sin.

                                        REFRAIN

(continued)

REFRAIN

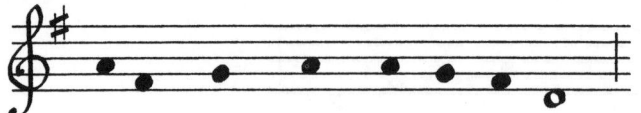

I ac - knowl-edged my sin to you,

and you for-gave me the guilt of my sin.

PSALM 32   TONE VII*b*

7 *There - fore* all the faithful will make their prayers
                    to you in time of tróu-ble;*
      when the great waters overflow, they sháll not
                    reách them.
8 You are my hiding-place;
      you pre-sérve me from tróu-ble;*
        you surround me with shóuts of de-lív-er-ance.

                                        REFRAIN

ALLELUIA - Ad libitum

PROPER 27 C

REFRAIN

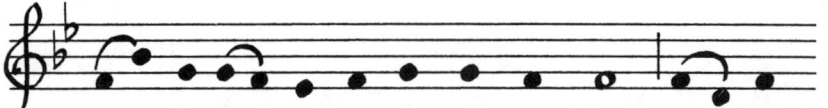

Keep me as   the ap-ple of your eye;   hide me

un – der the sha-dow of   your wings.

PSALM 17   TONE VIII*g*

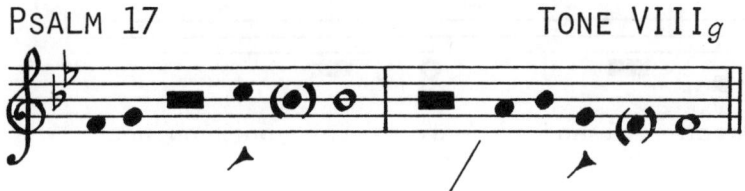

1   *Hear my* plea of innocence, O LORD;
     give heed to my crý;*
          listen to my prayer, which does not / come
                              from lý-ing lips.
2   Let my vindication come forth from your prés-ence;*
     let your eyes be / fixed on jús-tice.

                                    REFRAIN

3   *Weigh my* heart, summon me by night,*
     melt me down; you will find no im – / pu-ri-tý in me.
5   My footsteps hold fast to the ways of your láw;*
     in your paths my feet / shall not stúm-ble.

                                    REFRAIN

6   *I call* upon you, O God, for you will án-swer me;*
     incline your ear to / me and héar my words.
7   Show me your marvelous loving-kínd-ness,*
          O Savior of those who take refuge at your right hand
          from those who rise / up a-gaínst them.

                                    REFRAIN

BCP, p. 600

Proper 27 C

Alleluia II

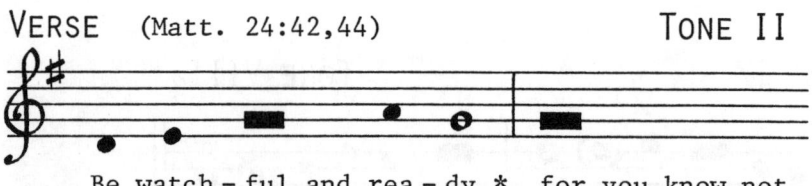

Al – le–lu–ia, al–le–lu–ia, al–le–lu–ia.

Verse (Matt. 24:42,44)   Tone II

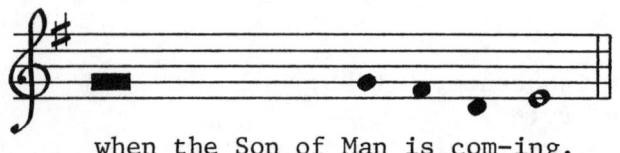

Be watch – ful and rea – dy,* for you know not

when the Son of Man is com–ing.

PROPER 28 C

REFRAIN

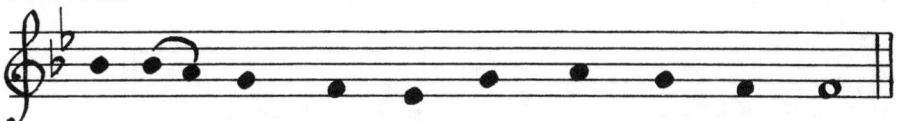

The Lord will judge the world with right-eous-ness.

PSALM 98   TONE VIIIg

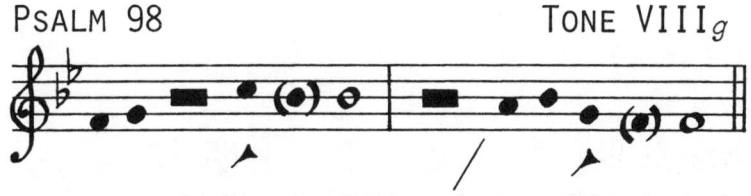

5   *Shout with* joy to the LORD áll you lands;*
      lift up your / voice, re-joíce, and sing.
6   Sing to the LORD with the hárp,*
      with the harp / and the voíce of song.

                                        REFRAIN

7   *With trum* - pets and the sound of the hórn*
      shout with joy be - / fore the Kíng, the LORD.
8   Let the sea make a noise and all that is ín it,*
      the lands and / those who dwéll there-in.

                                        REFRAIN

9   *Let the* rivers cláp their hands,*
      and let the hills ring out with joy before the LORD,
      when he / comes to júdge the earth.
10 In righteousness shall he júdge the world*
      and the peo - / ples with é-qui-ty.

                                        REFRAIN

PROPER 28 C

ALLELUIA I

Al-le-lu - ia, al-le-lu - ia, al-le - lu-ia.

VERSE (Rev. 2:10)   TONE If

Be faith - ful until death, says the Lord,*

and I will give you the crown of life.

PROPER 29 C

REFRAIN

The Lord of hosts is with us;

the God of Ja-cob is our strong-hold.

PSALM 46   TONE VIII*g*

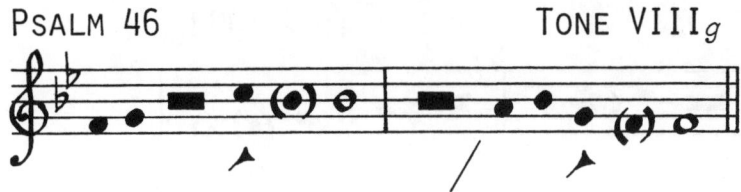

1 *God is* our refuge and stréngth,*
    a very present / help in tróu-ble.
2 Therefore we will not fear, though the eárth
                be moved,*
    and though the mountains be toppled into
              the / depths of thé sea;
3 Though its waters ráge and foam,*
    and though the mountains tremble / at its tú-mult.

                                REFRAIN

5 *There is* a river whose streams make glad the
                city of Gód,*
    the holy habitation / of the Móst High.
6 God is in the midst of her;
    she shall not be ó-ver-thrown;*
    God shall help her / at the bréak of day.
7 The nations make much ado, and the kingdoms are
                shák-en;*
    God has spoken, and the / earth shall mélt a-way.

                                  REFRAIN

(continued)   *BCP, p. 649*

REFRAIN

The Lord of hosts is with us;

the God of Ja-cob is our strong-hold.

PSALM 46   TONE VIII*g*

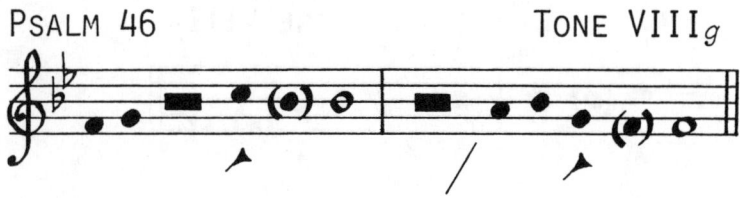

9   *Come now* and look upon the works of the LÓRD,*
      what awesome things / he has dóne on earth.
10   It is he who makes war to cease in áll the world;*
      he breaks the bow, and shatters the spear,
      and / burns the shíelds with fire.
11 "Be still, then, and know that Í am God;*
      I will be exalted among the nations;
      I will be ex - / alt-ed ín the earth."

                                        REFRAIN

PROPER 29 C

ALLELUIA VII

Al-le-lu - ia, al - le - lu - ia, al - le - lu-ia.

VERSE (Mark 11:10)   TONE VIIb

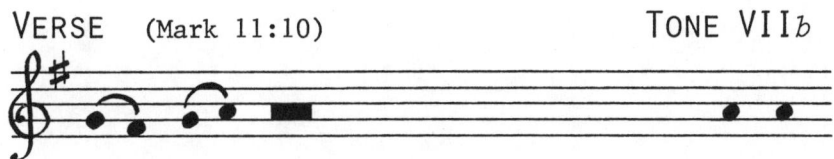

Bless - ed   is the kingdom of our father Da-vid

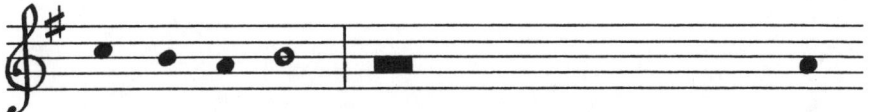

that is com-ing;* blessed is he who comes in the

name of the Lord.

Alleluia Verses

Ad Libitum

ALLELUIA VERSES

For use *ad libitum* when appointed in the Proper.
Any of the verses appointed for particular days
or seasons may also be used, provided that it is
congruent with the Gospel Reading which follows.

1. Show me your ways, O Lord;*
   lead me in your truth and teach me.   *(Psalm 25:3,4)*

2. I will bless the Lord at all times;*
   his praise shall ever be in my mouth.   *(Psalm 34:1)*

3. Your love, O Lord, for ever will I sing;*
   from age to age my mouth will proclaim
   your faithfulness.   *(Psalm 89:1)*

4. Sing to the Lord and bless his Name;*
   proclaim the good news of his salvation
   from day to day.   *(Psalm 96:2)*

5. The commandments of the Lord are sure;*
   they stand fast for ever and ever.   *(Psalm 111:7,8)*

6. Open my eyes, O Lord,*
   that I may see the wonders of your law.   *(Psalm 119:18)*

7. Give me understanding, O Lord,*
   and I shall keep your law with all
   my heart.   *(Psalm 119:34)*

8. Your word is a lantern to my feet*
   and a light upon my path.   *(Psalm 119:105)*

9. The Lord is faithful in all his words*
   and merciful in all his deeds.   *(Psalm 145:14)*

10. How good it is to sing praises to our God;*
    how pleasant it is to honor him with
    praise.   *(Psalm 147:1)*

11. Worship the Lord, O Jerusalem;*
    praise your God, O Zion.   *(Psalm 147:13)*

(continued)

12. Man shall not live by bread alone,*
    but by every word that proceeds from
    the mouth of God.   *(Matt. 4:4)*

13. Your words, O Lord, are spirit and life;*
    you have the words of everlasting life. *(John 6:63,68)*

14. The word of the Lord stands fast for ever;*
    his word is the Gospel preached to you. *(1 Peter 1:25)*

Ad Libitum 1 - Psalm 25:3,4

Alleluia II

Al - le-lu-ia, al-le-lu-ia, al-le-lu-ia.

Verse   (Psalm 25:3,4)   Tone II

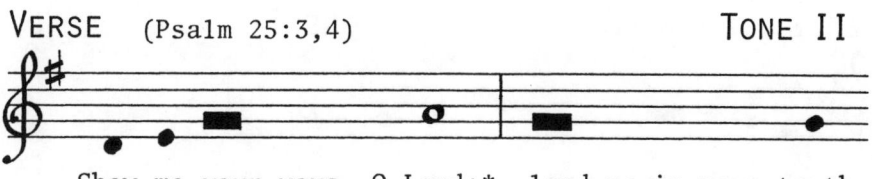

Show me your ways, O Lord;*   lead me in your truth

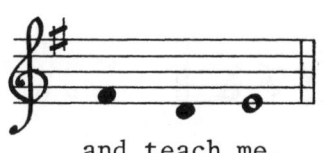

and teach me.

AD LIBITUM 2 - PSALM 34:1

ALLELUIA I

Al-le-lu - ia, al-le-lu - ia, al-le - lu-ia.

VERSE (Psalm 34:1)   TONE I*f*

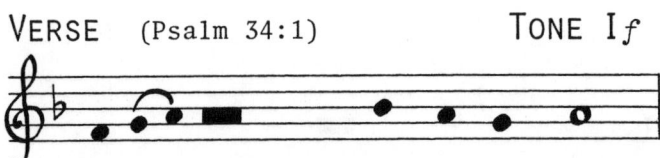

I will bless the Lord at all times;*

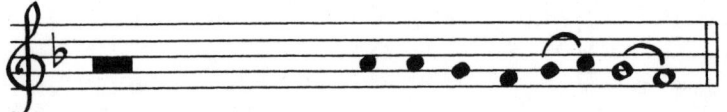

his praise shall ev-er be in my mouth.

Ad Libitum 3 - Psalm 89:1

Alleluia V

Al-le-lu-ia, al-le-lu - ia, al - le - lu-ia.

Verse (Psalm 89:1)   Tone V$_\alpha$

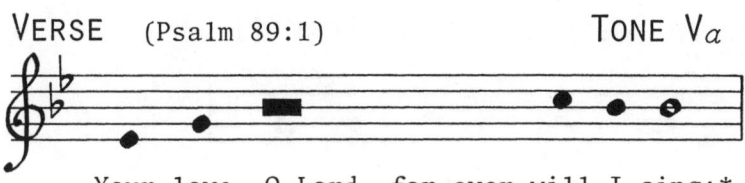

Your love, O Lord, for ever will I sing;*

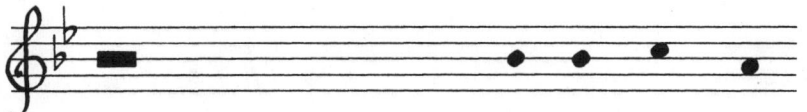

from age to age my mouth will pro-claim your

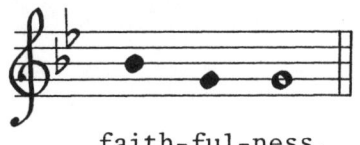

faith-ful-ness.

AD LIBITUM 4 - PSALM 96:2

ALLELUIA II

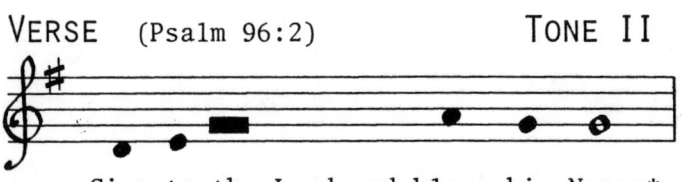

Al - le-lu-ia, al-le-lu-ia, al-le-lu-ia.

VERSE (Psalm 96:2)   TONE II

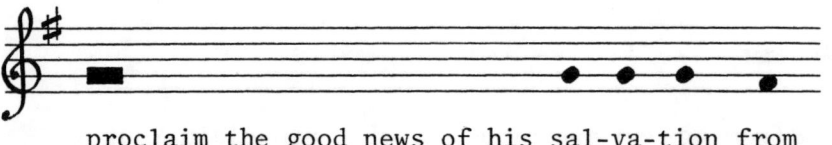

Sing to the Lord and bless his Name;*

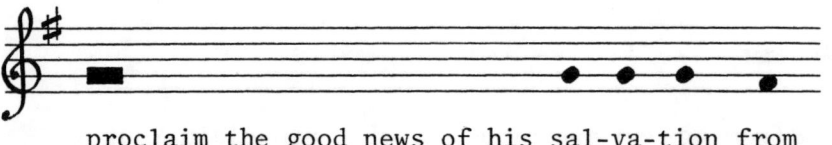

proclaim the good news of his sal-va-tion from

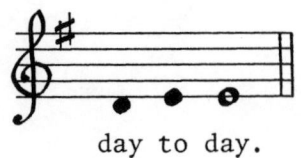

day to day.

AD LIBITUM 5 - PSALM 111:7,8

ALLELUIA VII

Al-le-lu - ia, al - le - lu - ia, al - le - lu-ia.

VERSE (Psalm 111:7,8)   TONE VII♭

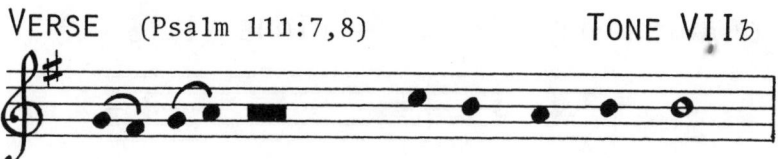

The   com - mandments of the Lord are sure;*

they stand fast for ev-er and ev-er.

ALLELUIA VIII

Al-le - lu - ia, al-le-lu - ia, al - le-lu-ia.

VERSE   (Psalm 119:18)   TONE VIII*g*

O - pen my eyes, O Lord,*   that I may see the

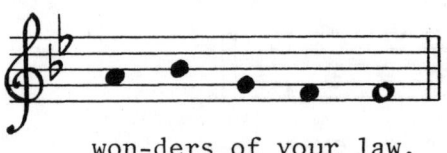

won-ders of your law.

ALLELUIA VI

Al-le-lu-ia, al - le-lu-ia, al-le - lu - ia.

VERSE (Psalm 119:34)   TONE VI

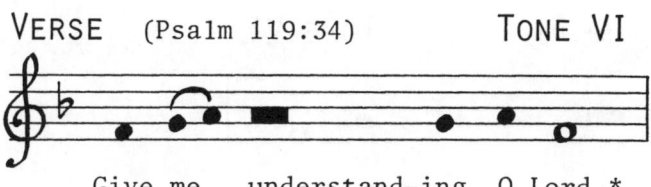

Give me   understand-ing, O Lord,*

and I shall keep your law with all my heart.

AD LIBITUM 8 - PSALM 119:105

ALLELUIA VI

Al-le-lu-ia, al - le-lu-ia, al-le - lu - ia.

VERSE   (Psalm 119:105)   TONE VI

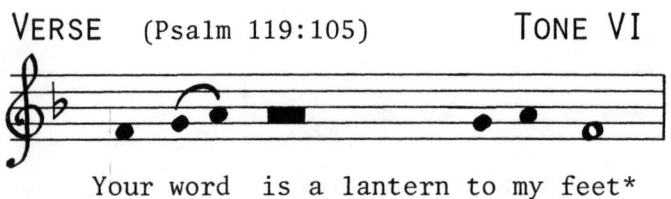

Your word is a lantern to my feet*

and a light up-on my path.

ALLELUIA III

Al-le - lu - ia, al-le - lu-ia, al-le - lu-ia.

VERSE (Psalm 145:14)   TONE III*a*

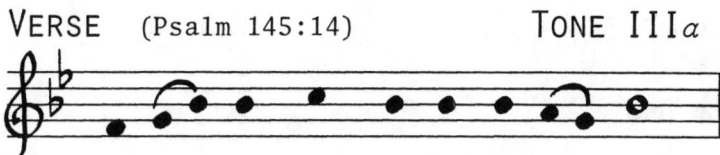

The Lord is faith-ful in all his words*

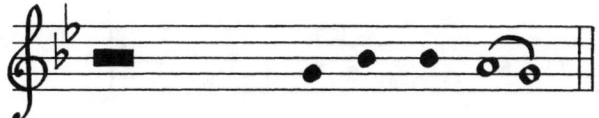

and merciful in all his deeds.

AD LIBITUM 10 - PSALM 147:1

ALLELUIA I

Al-le-lu - ia, al-le-lu - ia, al-le - lu-ia.

VERSE (Psalm 147:1)   TONE I*f*

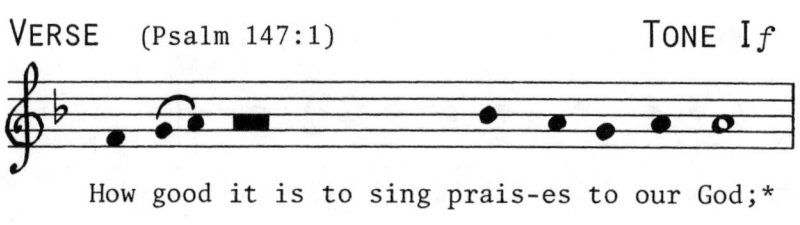

How good it is to sing prais-es to our God;*

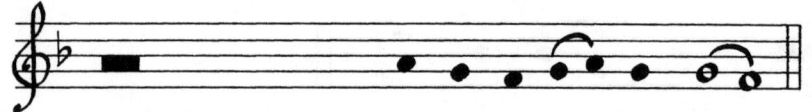

how pleasant it is to hon-or him with praise.

Ad Libitum 11 - Psalm 147:13

Alleluia IV

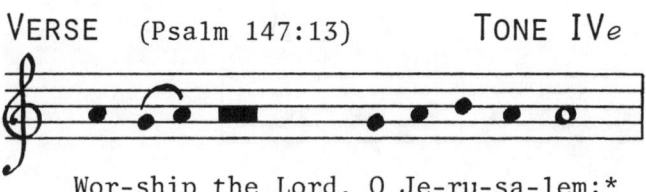

Al-le-lu-ia, al-le - lu - ia, al-le - lu-ia.

Verse (Psalm 147:13)   Tone IV*e*

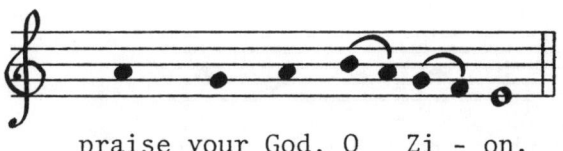

Wor-ship the Lord, O Je-ru-sa-lem;*

praise your God, O   Zi - on.

AD LIBITUM 12 - MATT. 4:4

ALLELUIA IV

Al-le-lu-ia, al-le - lu - ia, al-le - lu-ia.

VERSE (Matt. 4:4)   TONE IV*e*

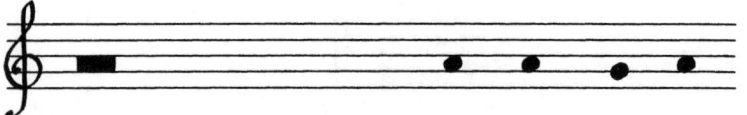

Man shall not live by bread a - lone,*

but by every word that pro-ceeds from the

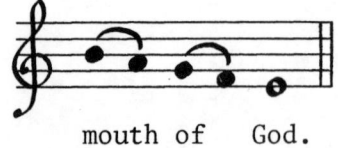

mouth of   God.

AD LIBITUM 13 - JOHN 6:63,68

ALLELUIA VII

Al-le-lu-ia, al-le-lu-ia, al-le-lu-ia.

VERSE (John 6:63,68)   TONE VII♭

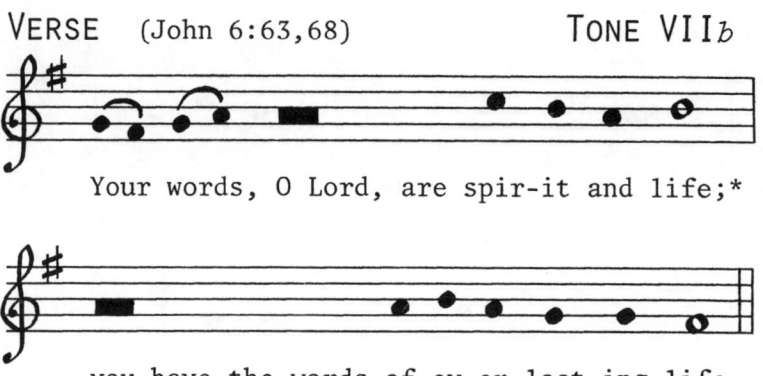

Your words, O Lord, are spir-it and life;*

you have the words of ev-er-last-ing life.

AD LIBITUM 14 - 1 PETER 1:25

ALLELUIA V

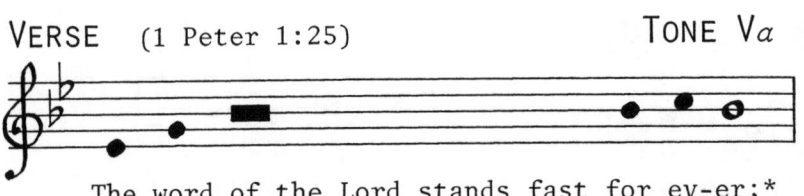

Al-le-lu-ia, al-le-lu - ia, al - le - lu-ia.

VERSE   (1 Peter 1:25)   TONE Vα

The word of the Lord stands fast for ev-er;*

his word is the Gos-pel preached to you.